Praise for *Heart & Mind Selling*

"*Heart & Mind Selling* is a must-read for any salesperson looking to connect with all levels of the customer's buying habits. But even more so, it provides a great look at understanding how different sales methods should be practiced in our constantly changing business world."

—**Phil Wilkins**, business owner, consultant,
and author of *Own Your Business, Own Your Life*

"This book is the key for sales professionals wanting to build authentic, trusting relationships with their customers. Sam's visionary Heart & Mind approach to selling is sure to generate quality customer interactions, increase client retention, and continuously improve your bottom line. *Heart & Mind Selling* is a must-have for anyone and everyone who wants to succeed in today's fact-paced business world."

—**Ken Wright**, The Wright Coach

"*Heart & Mind Selling* is an essential read for business people from all industries and all walks of life. Sam's techniques touch on emotional and logical levels. This book will give you the tools to meet your goals not only in your professional life, but in your personal life as well."

—**Juanell Teague**, consultant, speaker,
and author of *The Zig Ziglar Difference*

Heart & Mind Selling

The New Secret to Closing the Sale
And Winning the Customer for Life

Sam Allman

Heart & Mind Selling

*The New Secret to Closing the Sale
And Winning the Customer for Life*

Sam Allman

Boston, Massachusetts
www.AcanthusPublishing.com

Published by Acanthus Publishing
a division of The Ictus Group, LLC
343 Commercial Street
Unit 214, Union Wharf
Boston, MA 02109

Printed in the United States of America
10 9 8 7 6 5 4 3 2 1

Publisher's Cataloging-In-Publication Data
(Prepared by The Donohue Group, Inc.)

Allman, Sam.
 Heart & mind selling : the new secret to closing the sale and winning the customer for life / Sam Allman.

 p. : ill. ; cm.

 ISBN-13: 978-1-933631-32-5
 ISBN-10: 1-933631-32-5

 1. Selling. 2. Sales personnel. 3. Success in business. I. Title. II. Title: Heart and mind selling

 HF5438.25 .A45 2006
 658.85

Cover Design: Anthony Manes
Interior Layout: Julie Reilly

Table of Contents

Foreword

Foreword By
Michael D. Brown, M.B.A.
www.themichaeldbrown.com

Selling in General

Selling can help in so many facets of your personal and professional life. Treat everyone like a customer that you want to sell a product, idea, action, and/or services to. It can be your spouse, your customers, your children, your co-workers, etc.

I was forced to learn the art of selling very early. Raised with ten brothers and sisters I quickly learned that negotiation was a means of survival. I found myself constantly negotiating and selling at the dinner table, on the playground, and on those boring rainy days when we were all stuck in the house. I learned I could not use the same tactics on all ten brothers and sisters. I could offer my oldest brother my chicken in exchange for his dessert with great success, but I could never convince my middle sister to exchange her meat for my dessert. She did not see the intrinsic value in this, nor did this exchange appeal to her emotions. So I had to present a more compelling value-adding scenario.

The main goal in any instance of selling should be to meet the customer's needs, otherwise you can forget about making a connection and closing the deal. When you establish a bond, you connect with a customer for life. It is this customer who will sing your praises to his friends, and his friends to more friends, and on and on.

The quicker you can figure out what kind of beneficial experience and feeling the customer is looking for and align that with your offering, the quicker you will close the deal. You also need to realize when your offering will not align with the experience that the customer is looking for. At this point it's time to move on.

Engagement is a major step toward helping the customer appreciate the value in you and the product you are offering.

Selling is about getting people to do what you want, because it is right for them. In order to be an effective sales person you have to sell with passion and conviction.

The Case for Reading Sam Allman's Book, *Heart & Mind Selling*

Want to be an average salesperson? Don't read Sam's book. If you want to rise above average and deliver top tier performance, get Sam's book.

Sam tells it like it is and is very candid in stating the facts about selling and customers. In his book he presents 40 years of trial, errors, and some profound success strategies that have been thoroughly tested. He presents a perfect synergy between empathy (heart of selling) and ego-drive (mind of selling) and goes into great detail about why this synergy is fundamental to becoming a successful sales person.

It's the approach that makes the difference.

Sam goes on to state that success in sales is a result of empathy and ego drive. To close the sale and build a lifetime relationship, you need the Heart, and you need the Mind.

It's not enough to just satisfy the customer. The aim should be to turn the customer into a loyal customer as soon as possible. This customer will, in turn, come back again and again. Most importantly, she will be a walking billboard for you, showcasing your level of expertise via word of mouth—the most powerful form of advertising. If you are not turning these consumers into loyal customers, then you will forever spin your wheels. Sam points out in his book that 88% of customers leave the store satisfied but never come back. Clearly, just giving good service is not enough.

To get a loyal customer, you have to make a connection in addition to making a sale. Traditionally we think of sellers as the car salesman, not realizing that we are always selling something ourselves (at work, at leisure, with our family). Sam's *Heart & Mind Selling* is a superb read for sales professionals, and non-sales professionals who are looking to influence at a deeper level. If you are having difficulties convincing your spouse to slow down on spending, get *Heart & Mind Selling*. If you can't get your children to get an A in Algebra, get *Heat & Mind Selling*. If you can't get that customer to buy the new Mercedes S-500, get *Heart & Mind Selling*. If you are waiting tables and can never upsell past the Caesar Salad, get *Heart & Mind Selling*. If you can't convince your boss that you deserve a raise, get *Heart & Mind Selling*.

Heart helps you understand the customers, and Mind helps you ask for the sales.

Contrary to popular belief, the Heart *is* necessary to gain sales. Though you might yield short-term unsustainable results when you don't pour your Heart into it, you will not build long-term relationships and customer loyalty. It is relationships and loyalty that keep your pockets lined with rewards. The more relationships and loyalty you can build, the less stress you will have to endure to meet ever-increasing sales targets and goals. Put your Heart and Mind into selling, and create walking billboards that will help you spread the word about the positive sales experience that you deliver to your customers.

Sam brilliantly shows the reader four paradoxes that can be finessed:

Low Heart/Low Mind
Low Heart/High Mind
High Heart/Low Mind
High Heart/High Mind

Every salesperson (remember we all become a salesperson at some point) should go through an honest assessment and identify his or her personal paradox. Sam, at the end, shows how the High Heart and High Mind is a winning solution (I couldn't agree more). This should be the goal of any salesperson who wants to move from a "paycheck to paycheck" lifestyle to a lifestyle of wealth creation.

Sam effectively presents robust solutions and techniques for salespersons who need to boost either their Heart or their Mind when selling. And he also offers a boost to those lucky few who are already High Heart and High Mind.

Sam clearly states that the key is strengthening both traits and finessing and camouflaging them until you have a perfect combination that connects with the customer.

Sam presents this piece of work in a very compelling manner. He actually takes you through a journey where real solutions are presented along the way, encapsulated in 40 years of proven sales strategies and techniques that work. During this journey, he weaves in different selling styles of people that readers can readily identify with as a reference point. At the end of the journey the litmus test is when the salesperson has moved the customers to not only make the purchase but to a point where they agreed to a life-long relationship.

When you read Sam's book, *Heart & Mind Selling,* you get a masterpiece:

$ You get the problem and the need

$ You get the step-by-step solutions to becoming a Heart & Mind salesperson

$ You get strategies and techniques backed up by 40 years of experience

$ You get the questions and framework to perform a valuable self assessment

This is not your normal sales book that provides the reader with a laundry list of hidden "secrets" to successful selling. Instead, Sam has written an exhaustive and comprehensive piece of work that addresses the foundation and fundamentals of successful selling that is the Heart & Mind combination.

How Heart & Mind Selling has Worked for Me Personally

I worked my way through college waiting tables at a high-end steak and seafood restaurant. Waiters (salespeople) would struggle to get customers to buy the more expensive items on the menu, which would lead to better tips as a percentage of sales. They would often wonder on slow nights in the restaurant why I would have a full section of customers and be making record tips. It was because I had a number of loyal customers who had turned into billboards (they were advertising for me even when I was asleep). On occasion, I had customers who couldn't dine in my section (because it was full) who would come up to me after their meal with another waiter and tip me. While waiters were scurrying around toward the end of the month to make enough tips to pay the rent, I was requesting days off. I had made enough during the first ten days of the month to meet my expenses plus some.

People constantly asked me, "Michael, how is it that you can get customers in the palm of your hand so rapidly and how is it that you rarely have to haggle with them about price? They just seem to instantly believe you and quickly make the decision!" I have attempted to explain to people that the secret lies within the initial connection that you make with customers, which connects to the experience in which they find value. They then get to a point where they're unable to imagine not doing what it takes to secure this experience (in this case, buy the products/services that I suggested). Coupled with all of this was the enormous amount of trust that my customers bestowed upon me to recommend the right items and deliver the perfect experience. Yes, you can be a top salesperson with ethics! The number of people who posed the question to me seemed to understand what I was saying, but many wanted me to write down the secrets of successfully connecting with the customer and the ease of moving them to a quick positive decision. Thanks to the work that Sam has done with *Heart & Mind Selling*, I will be handing them all a copy of this well thought-out book. His book eloquently presents the answers to so many sellers' questions that I know it will grow and save sales careers!

Introduction

I started in retail over 50 years ago. My dad sold and installed carpet. Later, he owned a carpet store. At 8 years of age, I would go along on installations to thread his needles and, when I was older, to cut and install the carpet. When I asked him why he brought me along, he said, "Because I'm lonely without you." Actually, he wanted me to learn to work hard. "I only expect you to work a half-day," he would say, "and I don't care which 12 hours it is." I was 16 when I made my first sale. Dad said, "Go to Mrs. Smith's house and show her some carpet samples. You know what to say. If you get confused, just remember that the fuzzy side goes up!"

Mrs. Smith pointed to one of the samples I had laid on her living room floor and asked, "Will this carpet show footprints?" In 1961, all carpets were loop…except the shag she had selected. Wanting to win this sale, I said, "No, it doesn't show footprints because it's shag. Better yet, you could nail the seams together and you couldn't tell! It won't show any-thing." (You know the joke: How can you tell when a salesman is lying? His lips are moving!)

Two weeks later, my dad and I were installing her shag carpet. She wasn't home and had left our check on the counter. I stood back to look at our finished work, and suddenly felt sick to my stomach. Footprints! I had lied to my customer to make the sale and was betrayed by hundreds of footprints.

Driving home, I was quiet. Dad suggested, "Why don't you call Mrs. Smith when we get home and see how she likes the carpet?" I said, "No! No! And don't you call her, either!"

Thus, my first sale violated the most basic rule: Selling is about getting people to do what you want because it's right for them. I had figured out the first part but totally missed the second!

Dad eventually decided I was too lazy for the carpet business, so he encouraged me to get a college education. I earned a bachelor's degree in microbiology and a master's in microbiology and biochemistry. I was within an inch of my Ph.D. when I learned how little my professors earned each year. That's when I quit school, opened my own carpet store, and got back into sales. I loved it. Soon I was selling a lot and earning way more than my professors.

Within a few years, I realized that my sales methods worked not just to sell carpet but also worked in my personal life. Selling now helps me persuade my neighbor to cut his grass and my son to clean his room. It helps me to remember to entice my beautiful wife to go out for a romantic evening because of another basic sales principle—and she'll do it for her reasons, not mine—I know I had better provide her (my best customer) with what she wants. As Peter Stark says in *The Only Negotiating Guide You'll Ever Need*, "meeting the needs of your counterpart is absolutely critical."[1]

If you meet my wife, you will know I'm a superior salesman. It's obvious that I oversold myself, and she undermarried. I married her after my first wife left me—after 18 years and five children. (One day, she hit me with the news that she wanted to eliminate stress from her life. Apparently, I was it!) Thankfully, I got custody of the children. When I met my current (and final) wife, I was 40 years old with five kids, and she was 26 with two. So when we married, she became the young mother of seven kids! Twenty happy years later, she's still with me. (I think it's because I've learned the importance of continued customer service and follow-up!)

After we married, I began working on my life's goal—to help others learn more effective principles of selling. I wanted to help salespeople improve their work, family, and community lives. I bought every book and audio-tape I could find on selling, human psychology, principles of influence, leadership, business management, customer service, and teaching. I gulped them down, and incorporated them into the selling, personal growth, and leadership seminars I teach and the books I publish. I still read everything I can get my hands on. I relish the opportunity to share what I've learned during five decades of studying and selling.

What do I want you to gain from my story?

The realization that everything is about selling! When you learn effective principles of selling at work, you can apply those same principles to enhance your personal life. Proper selling methods bring people together because the seller's motives are the buyers' best interests: "Your wish is my command!"

Selling need not be boring. When you connect with each customer's Heart and Mind (instead of pushing products), selling brings joy. You gain new friends, and people are infinitely more interesting than carpets.

Sales skills and techniques can be learned, but few people develop the patience and humility to learn them. Sales and motivation expert Brian Tracy says, "The average salesperson never reads a book on selling. That's why he/she is average."[2] Because you're reading this book, you won't be average.

This book distills the sales skills and secrets I have spent my life learning. These habits have taken me to new heights as a salesperson, both in reputation and income. I'm confident they can do the same for you. I know how tough it is to sell day after day, year after year. But I believe your increased sales generated by using the Heart & Mind Selling method will uplift you...and your bank account.

Sam Allman
August 1, 2006

Part I. The Heart & Mind Philosophy

In this section, you'll be introduced to the Heart & Mind Selling method and learn why it's an effective approach for increasing sales and maximizing customer loyalty.

Chapter 1

Are You a Heart or Mind Salesperson?

"When Heart and Mind work together, expect a masterpiece."

—Sam Allman

A 1964 *Harvard Business Review* article by David Mayer and Herbert M. Greenberg ("What Makes a Good Salesman?")[3] reported that after studying 7,000 salespeople, the top two characteristics of peak performers were empathy and ego-drive.

Empathy is the understanding of and appreciation for your customer's emotions, needs, and experiences. *Ego-drive*, by contrast, is the desire to work to produce a result by influencing or even controlling others. Empathy works to match one person's understanding with another's. Ego-drive works to change another's understanding. The problem is that the tactics of each of these characteristics seem to be in conflict with each other.

So how do we reconcile these two seemingly opposing styles to come up with the peak performers Mr. Mayer and Mr. Greenberg identified?

That is what Heart & Mind Selling is all about. Heart & Mind Selling is a system I've created to teach you how to develop a perfect synergy between empathy (what I call the Heart of Selling) and ego-drive (what I call the Mind of Selling), so you can create an instant and lasting connection with every customer *and* close the sale. It is based on over 40 years of researching why customers buy and don't buy from certain kinds of salespeople. It is also based on my over 40 years of personal experience selling to customers on the floor, learning from trial and error, and then teaching my techniques to other salespeople like you.

What I've learned from my experiences is that we all have degrees of Heart and Mind within us, but only the top performing salespeople have discovered a way to finesse them both. What happens when we try to engage customers without a balance of empathy and ego-drive? Let me give you a few examples.

Rodney the Love Bug

When I was a floor covering salesman, I had a young salesman working for me named Rodney. Rodney was the nicest, sweetest salesman you ever met. He knew how to start a conversation with anyone. He listened. He asked questions. He made each customer feel like she was the most special person in the world (and she is!). He did everything right, except one thing: He couldn't close the sale.

Like many salespeople, Rodney had Heart up the wazoo, but scored a big zilch in the Mind department. He had unbelievable skill for understanding exactly what the customer wanted and communicating that, but when it came time to asking for the sale, he literally started to sweat. He thought selling was all about making people feel good. Of course, he was right…and he was wrong. Sales is about making people feel good to close the sale. The good news is I never had to fire Rodney. He fired himself because he was starving and couldn't pay his bills!

If you can relate to Rodney's situation, you have plenty of excellent skills to build on. You have a knack for getting people to like you and you've probably been this way since you were born. You've probably also experienced how this skill is a blessing and curse—you want to be loved so much and don't want to be pushy, that you feel bad or awkward when it's time to get down to business. You literally fear asking people to take the steps needed to make the sale. That's a problem for obvious reasons, least of which is the sales manager breathing down your neck. But most likely you're not a total love bug, or else you probably would have quit or been fired long ago.

The problem with love bugs is simply that they don't know how to be anything but a love bug. They don't have an egoistic bone in their bodies and their parents probably taught them nice things like you shouldn't be selfish or you should always put principle before profit. Those are good things in some professions, but in the competitive world of sales, that approach just won't work.

If you are an extreme love bug like Rodney and you really do want to make it in sales, don't worry. You're not alone and you don't have to be this way forever.

Charlie the Closer

Then there are those salespeople who have the opposite problem: They're too darn pushy and not loving enough.

A few years ago, my niece asked me if I would go shopping with her for a new car. As a man, I guess she thought I would be an expert at these kinds of things—and maybe she thought that, with my sales experience, I would be able to see through the sales talk and help her get her a fair price. Anyway, I said I would go.

When we got to the dealership, we started looking at some of the cars and sticker prices on the windows. We were approached within five seconds by Charlie, one of the salesmen on the lot. He was a short fellow with jet black hair and a slick suit. I don't know why, but immediately I didn't like this guy. He reminded me of many of the sales professionals I've encountered over the last 40 years, working in furniture stores, cell phone booths in the shopping mall, and financial service companies across the country.

"Would you like to test drive one?" Charlie asked, looking at me.

"Actually, she's the one buying the car," I said. "Maybe you should ask her."

My niece had her eye on a nice black convertible and said she'd like to take it out for a spin. He went inside and came back with the keys. In a few moments we were racing up the hill with the top down and the dealer in the passenger's side.

When we got back, the dealer invited us into the office to discuss price.

"This is one of our top sellers. We can barely keep them on the lot…but, because I like you," he said, "I'm prepared to make a fair offer. How about $22,000?"

"Actually," I interjected, "We were looking for something closer to $17,000…"

The salesman shot me a look like he was about to stab me. It's that leveling gaze my wife uses when she is unhappy with me.

"Are you buying the car? Then why don't you stay out of it and let us talk about the price."

I bit my tongue and let Charlie shoot himself in the foot. He did all the wheeling and dealing you would expect, and after about ten minutes of telling her why he couldn't drop the price, he pulled the old "Let me talk to my manager trick." That was our cue to escape. And we did.

The problem with closers like Charlie is that they're hardwired only to close the sale, which isn't a bad thing, except when you have a customer who wants a softer, more loving approach (which is almost every customer!!!). Closers *close* plenty of sales and make lots of money—and they write books where they disclose their closing secrets. Of course, what they don't tell you is what happens after the sale. Have you ever bought something because you wanted it, even though the salesperson was a jerk? Have you ever bought something because you felt embarrassed or pressured? Of course. We all have. The closer feels happy because he closed the sale. The boss feels happy because Charlie just created another "satisfied" customer. But how satisfied is she? You can almost guarantee that customer is never coming back to Charlie again. If you're a sales manager or business owner, that's a problem. And if you're Charlie, that's a problem too. According to a recent study conducted by The Gallup Organization, over 88 percent of customers leave the store "satisfied" but never come back.[4] That's a sign that traditional closing skills alone are failing to capture the loyalty that is so key to doing business in today's Internet, bargain basement, Wal-Mart® sales environment. It also means you have to work harder; i.e., you have to constantly struggle to find new customers.

Again, if you're a closer like Charlie, you have 50 percent of what it takes to be a perfect salesperson. You have the Mind, now you only need the Heart.

To see the big picture of the selling process, let's review the time-tested sales pyramid:

Relative Time & Effort to Invest in Each Stage of Selling

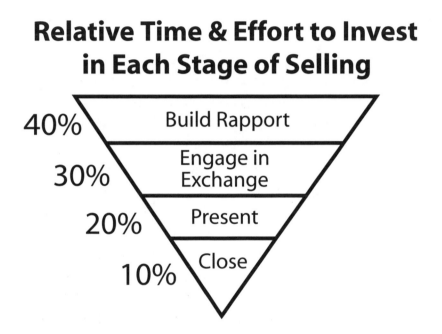

Chapter 2

Finessing the Paradoxes of Heart & Mind

"The opposite of a correct statement is a false statement, but the opposite of a profound truth may well be another profound truth."

—Niels Bohr (1885-1962),
winner of the 1922 Nobel Prize in Physics[5]

Both the love bugs and the closers are just different sides of the same coin. They are paradoxes—two occurrences that seem to contradict each other but ultimately work hand in hand. The trick as a salesperson is to learn how you can finesse those contradictory aspects into the ultimate sales personality and approach. In other words, you need to combine the ego-drive and the empathy to close the sale and build the lifetime relationship. You need the Heart, *and* you need the Mind.

If you want to close more sales, you need the Mind to ask for them. You also need the Heart to understand customers' needs and work in collaboration with them to help find a solution, at a pace that works for them. If you want to build a loyal customer relationship, you need the Heart to express your care and concern on the deepest level, and you have to be well-liked. Customers don't come back to buy from people they don't like. At the same time, you have to unleash your Mind to set and achieve lofty goals and make your quota. There's no relationship to build unless there's some profit and benefit for both sides involved. The fact is these two characteristics are complementary; they complete each other.

To give you example of how you can finesse these paradoxes, let's look at how different salespeople with different degrees of Heart and Mind might handle the typical customer objection "I need more time to decide."

- ♥ **Low Heart, Low Mind**: The other name for this type of person is a "clerk." They are getting paid minimum wage to work behind a counter and boy, does it show. They're typically just order-takers and they generally don't care if the sale is made or not made because they have very little to gain either way. They don't try very hard to understand their customers or build an emotional connection and they are generally unmotivated when it comes to closing the sale. When a customer says, "I need more time to decide," their response is usually (only in their heads, we hope) "I don't care. It doesn't bother me. Come back when you're ready. Maybe I'll be working that day, maybe not." The result is that almost no customer loyalty is ever gained because no meaningful contact with the customer occurs. At the slightest whiff of resistance, these salespeople always give in and give up. And how much do they make? They make minimum wage.

- ♥ **Low Heart, High Mind**: These are the used car salesmen, the crazy closers. They are the guys who use lines like, "Is there anything I can interest you in?" or "If you find something today, would you be in a position to buy?" Their instinct is always to push the sale forward, with or without your emotional buy-in and they can get very frustrated if you show any resistance. When a customer says, "I need more time to decide," their response is usually, "What's there to think about? The price is going up tomorrow. I have three people looking to buy this, and you're never going to get a deal like this." This type of salesperson doesn't care about the customer and while their hard sale tactics might close the sale, they will ultimately destroy the customer relationship. If they make the sale, they will never sell to the customer again.

♥ **High Heart, Low Mind**: These are the love bugs—the salespeople who care about the customer relationship but are afraid to push enough to close the sale. When a customer says, "I need more time to decide," their response is usually, "I totally understand. It's a big decision and I want to make you happy, so here's my card and when you're ready to buy, call me." What typically happens is that the customer does buy, but from another salesperson. Salespeople with high Heart, low Mind generally take customer resistance at face value. They lack the skills, the ability, and often the will to ask questions to reveal the cause of the resistance or indecision. Therefore, they generally lose the sale. If they just pressed a little bit harder in a non-pressure way, they would realize how easy it is to overcome customer resistance.

♥ **High Heart, High Mind:** The Heart & Mind salespeople. Look at how this type of salesperson carefully finesses the situation. When a customer says, "I need more time to decide," their response is usually, "I totally understand. It's a big decision and I want to make you happy." So far the conversation is entirely like what the high Heart, low Mind salespeople would say, except the Heart & Mind salespeople don't give up on the sale. Instead, they camouflage their Mind with Heart. They might then say, "To help me understand how I can better serve customers, it's important for me to understand why you want to put off this decision. Is there a reason why you feel this way?" If the customer says it's because she's uncertain about price or about color, Heart & Mind salespeople can now work to resolve the customer's objection, whereas the high Heart, low Mind salespeople would never know why the customer didn't buy. Notice the difference. When used car salesmen try to resolve objections, it just seems too pushy. But when Heart & Mind salespeople do it, the nature of their actions and words communicate to the customer that her interests, not their own, are first in their minds. Every Mind-driven technique a Heart & Mind salesperson uses is skillfully camouflaged with Heart. For example, a Heart & Mind salesperson calls up a customer who is taking a long time to make a buying decision and says, "Mrs. Smith, I was thinking of you today. Is this a good time to talk?" (Notice the Heart & Mind salesperson asks for permission.) "I was thinking of you because I know you are making an important decision in a couple of days and I just want to know if there is anything I can do to help with your decision." The Heart & Mind salesperson is opening the relationship and moving the sale forward, without creating resentment.

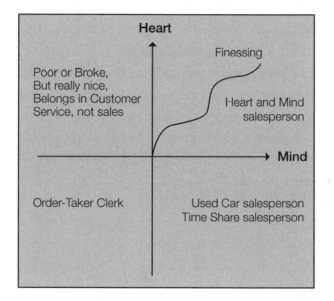

The Key Is to Camouflage

Heart and Mind are traits you have inside you to some degree already. If you didn't have some Heart, or empathy, you would be the least liked person in the world because you would literally not be able to understand, sympathize, or relate to anyone. People would talk and you wouldn't listen.

If you didn't have Mind, or ego-drive, you would never get anything done. You'd never stand up for yourself, or get in an argument, or tell someone what was on your mind, or ask for a raise. You would be a complete wash out in life—a feather blowing in the wind to whatever direction it sends you.

The key is strengthening both traits and finessing and camouflaging them until you have a perfect combination that connects with the customer.

Developing Your Heart Muscle

Some people have Heart by intuition. They can meet people for the first time and instinctively know where they're coming from, how they see the world, and how they're going to react to certain types of information. A good example of a natural Heart salesperson is Bill Clinton. Put Bill Clinton in a room of strangers and he will be able to make friends with anyone. After all, one of his favorite phrases was, "I feel your pain."

A good Heart salesperson, like Clinton, gets an intuitive read on people that allows him or her to build bridges between different ways of seeing the world. It makes sense then that Heart connections are strongest between those who share the same backgrounds and points of view. For example, having grown up in the western United States my entire life, I can immediately empathize and relate to anyone from the West a lot more than I can with someone in the East. We have certain shared ways of seeing the world, based on culture, that make it easier for us to understand each other, or connect Heart to Heart. In fact, you see this phenomenon all the time in politics. The man or woman who gets elected is usually the person voters can empathize with the most.

But there are also people who have developed Heart just like they would any muscle or skill. Heart is just another word for the ability to understand people and use that understanding to form an emotional bond. Empathy produces a connection between two people. There are always ways to increase your understanding of people and your ability to connect with them. You start by getting to meet and know more people, observing their behaviors, and making a mental calculation of what separates one person from another.

I had the opportunity to hone my observation skills all the time on the sales floor. I noticed that some customers were very forthright and direct with what they wanted. They were the customers who come up to you and say, "This is what I'm looking for, this is what I'll pay, now go get it." Then there were the customers who had trouble making up their minds. They aimlessly floated around for a while, picked something up, put it down, and then moved on. When you finally did approach them, they almost seemed as though they were not there to shop, just to hang out and have a conversation.

It wasn't until I read a few books on human behavior that I realized scientists had been studying the differences between people for years and had started classifying people according to personality styles. I used much of this research to help me create my own system for understanding the buying personalities of different customers. I call the system the 4 E's. I will talk more about the 4 E's in Part III, but I mention it here to show you that there are ways to increase your Heart levels by understanding people's motivations. There are also proven psychological techniques you can use to enhance your Heart connection with customers. I call them the 7 Laws of Influence because unlike personality types, they're universal. They trigger something that is deep and instinctual in all of us and are subtle enough not to make people feel like they're being manipulated.

Heart & Mind Selling gives you many techniques you can use to develop your Heart muscle. But having Heart is just one piece of the puzzle. You also need to communicate it. That's why the book also discusses ways to do that and how to work this technique into your sales approach to camouflage Mind and create a stronger emotional connection.

Developing Your Mind Muscle

There's a scene in the movie *Glengarry Glen Ross*[6] when Alec Baldwin's character, Blake, reminds the salespeople of the A.B.C's: "Always Be

Closing." That's how people with a strong amount of Mind approach the world. They always have the end in sight and they do whatever it takes to get there. You meet salespeople and businesspeople like this all the time. Talk to them about anything but results and the bottom line, and they'll stop listening and their eyes will glaze over. Who knows, maybe you're like that!

Like Heart, some people are born with enough Mind to share with the entire world. I'm thinking of someone like Donald Trump. He's always focused on the next sale, on the next project, and on the next big deal, and if you slow him down or stand in his way, watch out: "You're fired." There's no doubt that Mind has been a tremendous asset for Trump. It is the force always moving him and you (hopefully) forward.

Maybe Mind is the missing piece of your puzzle? Mind, like empathy, can also be developed with practice. How? Well, Mind is just another name for selling skills. You've probably been taught selling skills at some time in your career or you learned them in one of those master sales books written by closers like Charlie. These are the techniques you use to move the sale along like:

- ♥ Matching people's body language
- ♥ Finding things you have in common; commenting on something on their desk
- ♥ Giving a sincere compliment
- ♥ Using their names
- ♥ Making sure you ask really good questions
- ♥ Setting stretch goals for yourself
- ♥ Developing a positive attitude about yourself

Again, Mind is limited without empathy to match. It's important to move customers forward, but while you may close the sale, if you don't do it at their pace, according to their natural preferences, you will create friction and resentment. That's why the key to Heart & Mind Selling is learning how to sell with the Heart *in* Mind. Understanding customers and communicating this understanding is not enough—you must carry it forward through the entire sales process or customers will quickly spot you as a fake, someone who's pretending to have Heart just to make the sale. That's why Heart & Mind salespeople know how to camouflage their Mind at all times with Heart.

Chapter  3

The Heart & Mind Customer

"People may think that their behavior is purely rational, but it rarely is. Twenty years of research in two very different fields— neuroscience and behavioral economics—has established quite clearly that people base their decisions on a complicated mixture of emotion and reason."

—John Fleming, Curt Coffman, and James K. Harter[7]

To recap so far: I've just explained the ingredients for a top performing salesperson, from here on known as the Heart & Mind Salesperson. You finesse Heart and Mind until you acquire the perfect combination for the customer with whom you are working. Maybe you now know a little better where you stand using this combination.

Are you a hard-charging closer or a softhearted love bug?

Well, it turns out that customers are also two-sided and that top performing salespeople take this into consideration and know how to finesse the paradoxes.

We know from science that human motivations can be boiled down to the two categories of reason and emotion:

- ♥ **Reason** derives from the cerebral cortex, the source of perception, judgment, learning, creativity, and logic. It is proactive.

- ♥ **Emotion** derives primarily from the limbic system. It is reactive.

Together, the emotional response from the limbic system and the rational action from the cerebral cortex compose a person's motivation, decision, and action. All this is just a fancy way of saying that human (and therefore customer) motivation is driven by emotional facets like feelings, fears, and frustrations as well as logical components like price, convenience, and reliability.

In the sales exchange, whether it's on the floor or through print in the form of marketing, a Heart & Mind salesperson will touch both sides of the customer's brain. In other words, he or she will present a product and service in alignment with the customer's emotional wants.

For example, if you were selling a sneaker to a 17-year-old kid, you might assume that the kid simply needs the sneaker because he wore the old ones out. But if you dig deeper through the process with deep listening and questioning, you may be able to capture his emotional want—that is, he wants to be able to jump higher than his friends on the basketball court. Speak to that want, and you will have his attention and his interest. You will have greased the wheels of the sale.

But there are also rational factors at play. Maybe the 17-year-old sees another pair of sneakers on the shelf and wants to know which pair is better. He thinks about how much buying these sneakers will set him back: "Will it keep me from being able to go to the movies tonight?" So, you see, the emotional factors are only one part of the equation. The salesperson must also offer answers and explanations that address the rational justifications customers use to tell the difference between competing products or to talk themselves out of delaying a purchase.

Most salespeople get the rational part but overlook the emotional needs of the customers. The other day, I received a beautiful brochure from a professional marketing firm trying to sell me marketing services for my company. They told me how long they had been in business, who their clients were, and the process they used to create their work, and they loaded it with testimonials and pretty pictures of businesspeople in suits. They made a pretty excellent *rational* argument for why I should do business with them. There was only one problem: I wasn't looking for a rational argument—I was looking for inspiration, I was looking for hope, I was looking for a company who understood my business problems and could tell me how they could help me, warmly, with passion, and by exciting my emotions.

Too often we receive junk mail and sales pitches that hit us over the head with facts and figures and reasons why we should buy, without first acknowledging our needs and emotional wants. This is an example of Mind selling without the Heart. This is a problem for salespeople who lack Heart, because the root of being able to target your customers' emotions comes from first having the skills to understand their emotions. Even the most logical and rational customers have emotional motivation for buying at some level. It may be harder for you to get them to reveal it, but it's there. Look harder.

When All Else Fails, Aim for the Heart!

Customers—really all people—have two motivations, emotional and rational, but they always lead with the emotional side of their brains. It's the reason why the best ads in the newspaper grab you right with the headline—the writers have done their homework on you and have found the words that appeal to your emotions. It grabs your attention by grabbing your Heart. As you read on, you may learn more about the product's features and who uses it and how much it costs, but the best ads lead with emotion. Price and testimonials are rational pieces that allow you to justify the purchase only after you've already fallen in love. We do this to ourselves all the time. We see an expensive jacket we want to buy because we know we'll look good in it, but we justify the purchase rationally by reminding ourselves that it is on sale or that it will be useful at an upcoming wedding.

As a salesperson, if you connect with the emotional side of your customer's brain first, you will be more likely able to close the sale. But emotion doesn't stop there. Emotion ultimately must be carried throughout the entire sales process by reinforcing the emotional wants and by demonstrating care and concern for the customer. Take the emotion out of the equation at any time and you create the "Yes that really means No." In other words, you create a customer who is satisfied logically by the purchase, but unsatisfied emotionally by the exchange. You gave the customer what she wanted, but you really didn't connect. You talked when you should have listened. Your body language and words were too aggressive. You didn't compliment the customer on the purchase or even thank her.

Ultimately, this is why so many salespeople and businesses succeed in creating satisfied customers but fail when it comes to creating loyalty. They close the sale, but they can't open the relationship. But who can afford to fail in creating loyalty today? Can you? Face it. Customers can buy what you sell anywhere—and probably cheaper—so you need an edge to get them to buy because they like you. This is the core of Heart & Mind Selling—giving the customer a reason to come back again. If you engage customers on an emotional level from the beginning to the end of the sale, you will capture their Heart for life. Buying from you is like visiting an old friend!

I like to use the example of the Chinese restaurant that my wife and I keep going back to. Sure, the food is good. That's the rational reason for our return visits. But plenty of restaurants have good food. We also keep going back because they know us, they always ask about our family, and we feel like they really *care*. This appeals to our Heart.

Loyalty is critical. In sales, it's what you strive for. It's the difference between the single purchase of a satisfied customer and the continuous purchases of a loyal customer who keeps coming back to buy more. Tap into your customers' Hearts and Minds and you'll have achieved the most essential ingredient for creating the endless sales relationship. You'll close the sale, and you'll open a relationship you can profit from continuously down the road.

Chapter  4

The Heart & Mind Advantage

"We must combine the toughness of the serpent and the softness of the dove, a tough mind and a tender heart."

—Rev. Martin Luther King, Jr.

In an age where the Internet and over-competition are killing our sales, I believe Heart & Mind Selling is your proverbial ace in the hole—the edge you need as a business owner and salesperson to create the kind of customer loyalty everybody is talking about but no one seems able to deliver. That's because Heart & Mind Selling addresses cultural, psychological, and social factors that affect the exchange between a customer and a salesperson.

The First Factor: Customers are more skeptical than ever of salespeople—it's getting harder and harder to win their trust.

Do you read junk mail? Do you buy from late night infomercials? Do you believe politicians actually keep their campaign promises?

As consumers and employees, we are increasingly skeptical of being sold. We have been trained to believe sellers are manipulating us or leaving out some of the facts. Unless we are shown that people have our true interest at heart, we won't be able to let our guard down and allow true loyalty to sink in. By showing you how to generate a sincere feeling of love and compassion for people and how to verbalize and demonstrate this actively to customers and employees, Heart & Mind Selling defuses natural skepticism and replaces it with an instant feeling of trust and openness to new ideas.

The second factor: Customers are hungry for understanding and attention, and the salesperson who can deliver this in droves will become rich.

Why do people spend $4.50 on a cup of coffee or espresso at Starbucks® when they could make their own coffee at home for two weeks for the same price? Why are bookstores like Barnes & Noble® and Borders® packed with people until 11 p.m. at night?

Thanks to the breakup of families and longer work hours, we feel increasingly isolated from people and communities and are not getting enough emotional satisfaction at home. Therefore we seek—in fact we demand—understanding from the other areas in our lives. We don't want shopping, for instance, to be just a transaction: We crave a dialogue that allows us to tell someone how we feel and then have those feelings valued and affirmed by the salesperson on the other end. By showing you how to understand your customers, Heart & Mind Selling allows you to capitalize on this modern sense of loneliness by delivering a meaningful experience to customers every time.

The final factor: Customers have shorter attention spans than ever and anything that isn't immediately relevant will be ignored.

When you want to buy a book or a movie, what do you do? You go on Google® or Amazon® and you punch in the title and...poof! Exactly what you want pops up on the screen.

Thanks to search engine technology and a consumer society obsessed with customization, we require things to be immediately relevant to us. We want things to bend to our will and we won't tolerate things that don't speak to us at our level. It's why traditional advertising is being replaced by search engine advertising. As salespeople, this means we have even less time to make information relevant to customers. We must be able to read the subtle hints from body language and verbal cues to know how to frame the sale, the pitch, the offer, or the command in a way that will be emotionally relevant. By showing you how to uncover the hidden motivations and needs of customers in seconds and teaching you how to adapt your selling style to the buying style of others, Heart & Mind Selling allows you to eliminate the resistance you create when you don't hit the mark and try to get customers to bend to your agenda.

A Final Word

Heart & Mind Selling is the main ingredient for developing a deeper emotional and psychological bond with your customers. And when you extend it to your customers and carry its spirit throughout your entire sales transaction, you become nearly unstoppable. Let's get started!

Part II.

Becoming a Heart & Mind Salesperson

In this section, we'll focus on the internal changes you need to make before you can build a Heart & Mind connection with every customer.

Chapter  5

Developing the Heart & Mind Attitude

"There is only one boss: the customer. And he can fire everybody in the company from the chairman on down, simply by spending his money somewhere else. Whether a person shines shoes for a living or heads up the biggest corporation in the world, the boss remains the same. It's the customer! The customer is the person who pays everyone's salary and who decides whether a business is going to succeed or fail."

—Sam Walton, founder of Wal-Mart®[8]

Several years ago, I interviewed the sales manager of Sears®'s top floor-covering salesperson. The salesman had quite an impressive track record, producing the most sales in the last *thirty* years! When I asked the manager why this salesman was so good, she said she didn't know for sure. Sears's management team had analyzed his sales techniques and couldn't pinpoint the reason for his success. The manager's comment to me: "His customers say he *really* cares."

I think there is a powerful lesson we can draw from this story: The best salespeople bring more to the table than just skills or techniques. They seem to possess intangible qualities that endear them to customers in ways that are hard to quantify, analyze, or even replicate in other salespeople (much to the chagrin of sales managers). I compare it to what separates a good musician from a virtuoso like Mozart or Jimmy Hendrix. While a good musician possesses the technical skills to play a piece of music flawlessly, even beautifully, a virtuoso's performance is simply unforgettable. For whatever reason, their performance touches you deeper. It has more soul. It stands out.

One of the intangible qualities top performing salespeople possess, as we discussed in the last chapter, is Heart—the ability to understand customers on an emotional level. But to achieve Heart and really connect with and understand your customer, you need to possess another intangible quality first, the supreme intangible quality represented by the salesman in the story above—you need to have the right kind of attitude. And not just any attitude, but the attitude of love towards your customers.

I know, I know, love is one of those yucky words that's becoming somewhat of a cliché in sales and customer service. We're constantly being told to *love our customers*. But the funny thing is, for all our talk, customers still don't feel loved.

In the 1950s, shoppers generally felt appreciated by the stores they frequented. By the end of the 20th century it became apparent that customer satisfaction had subsided. Today, customers are more likely to defect than ever. If your business could just keep a small percentage of these customers from deserting, you could boost profits by a huge margin!

The major reason for this steep decline in customer loyalty is the refusal of many companies to meet their customers' expectations. In a world where most customers are not treated as VIPs, people will shop where their self-esteem, patronage, and ideas are appreciated and enhanced.

For many shoppers, having their minimal expectations met is not enough. When buyers hear a mechanical "Thank you for shopping," or a salesperson approaches them but obviously doesn't care, shoppers go elsewhere, looking for that little extra feeling of L-O-V-E. You need to find out what that means to each customer. Only customers who feel your love and loyalty to them individually become customers for life. Only customers who feel *loved* every time you see them will stay in your buyer/seller relationship.

As much as I hate to repeat something you're probably tired of hearing, loving your customer is really the glue that holds the Heart & Mind Selling approach together. And you might as well stop reading the book unless you take this to heart.

Defining Love in the Sales Equation

"Loving your customers?" you might say. "What a strange concept. You mean I have to buy them candy and flowers? Or get down on one knee and ask for their business?"

Well, no…and yes. Of course, I'm not suggesting you have to walk around on bended knee like a lovesick suitor. I'm really talking about loving your customers the way you would anyone you want to become closer to—putting them first in your mind, thinking about how to make them happy, being considerate and loyal, giving them reasons to trust you, listening. And a small gift now and then couldn't hurt. Loving is all about giving.

Love, in its simplest form, is caring about, treasuring, and appreciating another person. Love means caring enough about someone else that you go out of your way to do special things for that person.

Loving in sales comprises any thought, word, or deed that enhances your customer's experience. Loving the customer is treating her with unconcealed moral sense—the motivation that derives logically from the ethical or moral principles that govern your thoughts and actions. It's letting your inner light show. We're going to discuss some of these beacons in the pages of this book: honesty, integrity, and loyalty. This idea of moral sense applies not just to salesmanship, but to your entire life.

I believe it's this *loving* of our customers—Heart coupled with visible appreciation and caring—that produces lifetime customers and consistently high sales. Note that *loving, empathy,* and *caring* are all active words—they must be done intentionally.

In my sales seminars, I ask, "What is the opposite of love?" Many people reply, "Hate." I disagree. If I *hated* you, at least I'd feel some emotion. I think the opposite of love is apathy. If I'm indifferent, I feel nothing toward you. I'd just as soon walk away from your store and never look back. When it's time to buy that item again, the customer won't even notice that your store is still there. My friend Jeff Disend, author of the book *How to Provide Excellent Service in Any Organization*, says that when he's an ignored customer, he declares loudly, "I hope they got a good look at my face—because they'll never see it here again!"[9]

My perception is that the number one reason for losing a customer is *perceived* indifference by you or your store. This sense of non-caring causes *far* more defections than a higher price.

Love will appear programmed, however, if it's not rooted in compassion or caring. Only when used together do those feelings bond one heart to another. When you connect to your customers by extending both Heart and compassion, they'll begin to feel safe. They'll reveal their wants—without fear of being criticized, compared, or abandoned.

Find me a person who knows how to love customers, who loves to serve people, who gets a true joy out of knowing more about others, and I'll show you a salesperson who, with great technique training, can become a peak performer. Get your Heart right and your Mind will follow.

What Are Your Motivations?

Why are you reading this book? Surely, you're looking for ideas that will help you become a better salesperson and make more money. But are you also concerned about your customers? Do you want to help people make buying decisions that truly benefit them and their families? Or are you only concerned with the short-term gain? In other words, what are your motivations for selling?

When we talk about love, what we're really talking about are your motivations and intentions for serving the customer. In other words, where's *your* Heart? In your wallet? Are you selling primarily to pay the bills? Or are you selling to serve? Does service deepen your life's purpose?

Salespeople whose motivations and intentions do not extend beyond their own needs never develop the long-term attitude needed to successfully maintain lasting relationships with customers. And their short-view attitude demonstrates itself to customers through their actions and words.

The great salespeople I have met are able to balance their short-term needs (i.e., hitting their numbers) with a long-term view of nurturing and caring for customers. Sometimes that means telling a customer that a product or service isn't right for her because you know that the customer is one hundred times more likely to come back to you with her other purchases if she trusts you to help her make the right decisions. In other words, great salespeople always have their customers' Hearts in the forefront of their Minds. They value integrity and trust. They care more about providing the right product than racking up sales. And they expect to make life-long customers—even generations of customers—by going the distance for them. The ultimate compliment you can receive as a salesperson is the customer's comment to management, "I'm not sure whether she works for you or me!"

It is this attitude of serving the customer, not selling to them, that best defines what love means in the sales equation and what is at the core of Heart & Mind Selling. If you love your customers, you are dedicated to their personal growth and development—not as customers, but as people.[10] You care about them when they're in your store, on the phone, or in front of your face—and you care about them even when they're not thinking about you. Wherever your customer goes, your Heart continues to go with them. You never stop looking for new ways to serve them and you serve them even if there isn't an immediate financial gain or upside for doing so.

I recently read in article in *Selling Power* magazine about a salesman who took off workdays and weekdays to help a customer search for his missing son. The same article mentioned another salesperson who actually extended a personal loan to help a customer get over a rough period in his business![11] These are two great examples of salespeople loving to serve customers.

But showing customers your love doesn't have to be this radical or extreme. For example, I experienced an act of love just last week. My wife and I were waiting for a table at one of our favorite restaurants. It was a very busy night and the hostess told us it would be approximately an hour wait before we sat down. An hour went by and still we hadn't been seated. Hungry and now very cranky, I approached the hostess again. "You said we'd have to wait for an hour before we got a table—it's now been an hour and fifteen minutes!"

The hostess could tell I was upset. Very calmly she asked, "Could I have your name again please?"

"Sam Allman," I said.

"*THE* Sam Allman?"

"Yes," I said with a little bit of surprise in my face.

"Well, Mr. Allman, I really apologize for the inconvenience. We've had an unexpected delay in some of our food service tonight and we hope you can understand if you have to wait another fifteen minutes. I promise it won't be any longer than that. As soon as you're seated we'll have the waiter come right over and take your order."

The hostess didn't know me, but for a brief moment she made me feel special and brought a smile to my face. Using love as her shield, she deflected my anger and converted into satisfaction.

It reminds me of a quote I like to use in my presentations: "Customers will forget what you did and forget what you didn't do, but they will never forget how you made them feel."

Heart & Mind salespeople make you feel like you're a million bucks, and they mean it.

Why Is Love So Important?

There are several reasons why it's absolutely critical you have an attitude of love towards your customer and why it's the glue that holds the Heart & Mind approach together:

1. Love helps you communicate sincerity, which is the glue of Heart &

Mind Selling. If you meet a customer and are focused only on closing the sale instead of serving her, you will communicate that intention through your words and actions. Even if you try to camouflage your Mind with Heart, you will not communicate the authenticity and sincerity to get customers believing your intentions are genuine and thoughtful.

It's like applying for a job you are qualified for but aren't passionate about—you may say all the right things in the interview and have the resume to support it, but the employer may get a gut feeling that you're putting on a show. Have you ever had that feeling about someone? I'm sure you have because we encounter insincere employees and salespeople all the time.

When you work consciously to shift your attitude from focusing on your needs to the needs of your customers, and you accept the attitude of humility and caring that goes with that, an amazing thing happens: All of your words and actions communicate sincerity. Your customers will sense that your motives and intentions are pure and they will open themselves up to trust and listen to what you say.

On the other hand, if you're reading this book just to learn some quick tips to close more sales and have no intention of learning how to better serve your customer, you have a long way to go before you will be able to communicate sincerity to customers. You will apply the techniques and closing skills in this book and your customers will see right through you. Learn to love your customers and you will have the intangible quality that communicates sincerity and trust with everything you do.

2. Love increases your closing rate. Love is mutual liking. It describes relationships characterized by mutual caring, support, respect, pleasant warmth, understanding, empathy, kindly interest, openness, and harmony.

I believe that your closing rate is driven, in large part, by the love you develop with a customer.

The first evidence for that belief is love's ability to touch the *core* of another person—the most protected and precious part. When we touch that part, we benefit from the Law of Love, sometimes called the Law of Affinity, which states that people buy from people:

- ♥ Whom they love
- ♥ Who love them
- ♥ Who understand them

In his recent book, *Clued In: How to Keep Customers Coming Back Again and Again,* Lewis Carbone establishes the value of carefully managing our customers' experiences.[12] He believes that customers decide whether the asking price is too high or just right by analyzing the product, services, people, and their own *feelings*. He says the buying experience is a "value proposition." He urges us to no longer ignore the patently obvious concept that the loyalty of our customers is "more a result of how customers *feel* about the overall experience they receive" than what they get in tangible items. With competitors constantly baiting your customers, you better offer an enticing experience…or they may be gone!

Except for rare loners, people *want* to relate to other people, to be loved, and to love them.

A second reason love raises closing rates is that it *humanizes* the process of buying a *thing*. With flooring, furniture, electronics, and other items for the home, buying is more than "a person attaching to a thing." It's a person attaching to another person, and *together* they attach to the best thing. Products are only *things*, but service is a *human* relationship. That's why customers value good service over products.

Casually we may say, "I *love* my car, my new TV, my computer." (No, I guess we *don't* often say we love our computer.) We have a right to *say* we love things, but we *can't* love things. By definition, love is an attraction to, and affection for, other people (and/or animals).

People connect to our *souls*. Products can't. *Things* can make tasks easier, delight the senses, secure us, appease our appetites, convey thoughts, and the like. They can please and satisfy, but not bestow emotions that leave lasting joy.

That's why I recommend you sell yourself in your first minutes with customers. Sell yourself *more* than the product. Sell *yourself* first, the *company* second, and the *product-service package* third (remembering to sell the emotional benefits at least as much as the rational benefits). More shoppers will buy when you sell in this order.

3. And finally, love helps us get outside our own framework and into the Hearts and Minds of customers. When you sell from a position of loving to serve your customers, you open yourself up to their needs and desires instead of focusing on yours. You accept the fact that it isn't about you—it's about the customer. This is the foundation of empathy—getting to the heart of your customer.

I think there's no simpler way to express this idea than The Golden Rule: "Do unto others as you would have others do unto you." But if you catch yourself falling into the trap of putting your needs ahead of the customer's and letting your ego-drive get in the way of empathy, here are some lines to repeat to yourself silently under your breath. Think of them as your Heart & Mind sales mantras:

- ♥ It's not about me, it's about the customer.
- ♥ How would I expect or like to be treated if I were the customer?

♥   What can I say or do for this customer to show her I care about her and not the sale?

Speaking the Five Languages of Love

It's not enough to feel love for your customers; you have to make your customers feel that you feel love for them. Customers know when you really care or love them—and they know when you don't. Again, it's about sincerity: When you don't have the attitude to match your skills, you can't create belief and the result is a disjointed picture. It's like wearing a $5,000 suit with $30 scuffed shoes to your next sales presentation—the whole thing just doesn't add up.

You have to communicate loud and clear through your words and actions. You can feel all the love in the world for your wife or husband, but if he or she doesn't know it, what's the point?

In fact, this is a second powerful lesson we can learn from the story of the top grossing Sears® salesperson at the beginning of this chapter. It's not as important that the salesperson cared for his customers as it is that his customers said he really cared. Think about that. By putting the emphasis on *really cared*, aren't they saying that other salespeople say or at least try to act like they care? Aren't they saying that salesman is a really good *communicator of love*?

Heart & Mind Selling is about teaching you how to communicate your love to customers. But there are some basic and simple things you can do right away to master this language. These are actions you can use to communicate your love to anyone from your customers to your kids. Gary Chapman gives them to us in his inspiring book *The Five Love Languages: How to Express Heartfelt Commitment to Your Mate.*[13] I find that he confirms why empathy underlies all great relationships, including sales relationships. As Chapman writes, the cement for all relationships is trust.

Whom do we generally trust? Those who understand us and value us. Our human need to love and be loved is so deep that its absence triggers our worst emotional pain and its presence floods us with joy. When someone feels understood, he or she thinks, "I've met someone who cares about me. I think I can trust this person."

When you act with empathy, your intent counts more than your technique. Each of Chapman's love languages allows you to give a person a different gift. I recommend that you learn them all, so you can speak the love language of all those people with whom you have relationships, both professional and personal. Chapman's five love languages are:

1. **Quality time.** People relish receiving focused attention. Have you noticed that great salespeople spend more time listening than talking? Because they sincerely listen, the customer never feels her time is wasted.

2. **Words of affirmation**. A compliment connects people. Isn't that one of the first things you offer someone you're interested in personally? Of course, words of affirmation extend beyond compliments. They include kind words, encouraging words, appreciating words, humble words, and respectful words. When people hear affirming words, they're far more likely to reciprocate and look for the good in *you*.

3. **Tangible gifts.** Simple gifts tell a story. Giving customers a soda, coffee, or bottle of water or sending a thank-you note announces that you care about them. Your very effort to secure the gift tells the customer, "This person was thinking of me." Of course, tangible gifts touch people more when combined with intangible gifts, such as your time, words, efforts, and actions.

4. **Acts of service.** This is the gift of effort, as my wife likes to call it. She feels loved when I take out the garbage without a reminder, or when I bring in the groceries from her car without being asked. People realize you care when you sacrifice your own interests to help them.

5. **Touch.** In all cultures, people greet each other by some form of touching. Touching and being touched connect us. It might be a firm handshake, a slight touch on the arm, or sometimes even a hug. Keeping yourself physically distant suggests that you're emotionally distant. Research shows that a restaurant server who touches the customer when delivering the check will receive a 34 percent increase in tips.[14]

Keep in mind that having Heart, as demonstrated in the five love languages, isn't a substitute for skills and knowledge. But if a person feels *secure* with you, she feels connected, and that invites a friendship. I think you'll see great improvement in all of your relationships when you incorporate the five love languages into them.

Developing Love for What You Do

How do you feel about sales? Do you love what you do?

It has been said that only a small number of workers are energized and engaged in work. And even more are just neutral—they show up and do what's expected but little more. The rest are disengaged. It's easy to blame customers, bosses, product offerings, or co-workers for this problem. But keep in mind, job *enjoyment* lies within your control.

If you don't love what you do, you won't be able to communicate love to your customers. It's as simple as that. American philosopher and humorist

Will Rogers said, "In order to succeed, you must *know* what you are doing, *like* what you are doing, and *believe in* what you are doing."

How do you know if you love your job?

When the alarm goes off in the morning, how do you feel about your job? Let's check the scale.

Think about what motivates you and what you most enjoy doing. List the positive and negative forces in your job. Can you eliminate any of the negatives? Enhance any positives? At the end of your evaluation, if selling appears to be your best vocation, start with a positive attitude and chances are you'll make the job more profitable and enjoyable.

There's an old story about two shoe salesmen who were sent to a remote island in the Pacific. One cables back, "Come get me. They don't wear shoes here."

The other cables, "Send me more shoes. No one has any." A good salesperson starts with a good attitude about the job, the product, and the customers.

To make your day more fun, write down five things you really enjoy doing at work that also strengthen the company:

1. _____
2. _____
3. _____
4. _____
5. _____

Now consider each one. How might you redesign your job to spend more time doing these tasks?

Finally, believe in what you're doing. Successful people don't work just to pass the time. They work to make a difference and get results. They also don't mistake working hard for getting results. If you take your car in for repairs and two days later the mechanic hands you a bill for labor and says he worked really hard but couldn't fix the problem, how would you feel about paying his bill?

Believing in your services and striving for results will set you apart from the average salesperson. Successful salespeople consider how they're benefiting the customer and derive personal happiness from knowing they've helped others. They love what they do because they love serving their customers.

And when you look at it that way, The Beatles were right: "All you need *is* love."

Chapter 6

Making Yourself More Trustworthy

"No virtue is more universally accepted as a test of good character than trustworthiness."

—Harry Emerson Fosdick (1878-1969),
American minister and author[15]

Trust is the underpinning element of every relationship, but especially the loving relationship you must build with each of your customers. Without trust, none of your actions or words will be believed. Trust is the bedrock of customer loyalty and increased closing rates.

Trust indicates mutual understanding, respect, credibility, and agreement. Trust is feeling and believing that someone is credible, reliable, understanding, good-willed, and amenable to joint leadership.

♥ **Credibility** is the power of inspiring belief. It is "belief-worthiness." Customers will test the accuracy of your knowledge of facts and definitions. They will assess your competence and evaluate your judgments and good sense. They will grant you credibility when you've proven it.

♥ **Reliability** is assurance of another's integrity. *Is he predictable? Can I rely on him?* Customers can answer yes when you've clarified the rules of your engagement and followed them. Then they can believe that you will do as you say and will not deceive or disappoint.

♥ **Understanding** is Empathy (see Chapter 8).

♥ **Good-will** is the motivation to serve another's interests—to be kindly disposed towards your customer.

♥ **Joint leadership** is the equal collaboration of you and your customer. Each of you brings your knowledge, experience, and judgment to the buying decision. The customer needs you to *lead* her to her options, but then she wants an equal voice in selecting the goods. She wants to feel that you want to guide her to find what's right for her.

But you must also trust the customer. Yes, *you* must play the trust game too. You have to let down your guard before she will let down hers. One-way trust doesn't last. Trust is nothing if not mutual—the buyer trusts the seller, the seller trusts the buyer. Remember, however, that your mutual trust must be sincere. Pretended trust will blow up in your face.

Trust is needed when two people have a shared objective, such as when you are selling and she is buying. Then you can get the customer to be "engaged to you" in the mutual objective—in this case, the product hunt.

Both of you must continuously work to avoid surprises and ensure predict-ability of the relationship.[16]

Therefore, a bond of trust with each customer will increase sales. Without it, we might as well be selling oceanfront property in Arizona.

How to Establish Your Trustworthiness

Customers will test your credibility with every claim you make. They'll be asking themselves these questions:

- ♥ Is the salesperson an authority on this subject?
- ♥ Is there a clear basis for his conclusion?
- ♥ Does he have a bias or vested interest?
- ♥ Do credible sources disagree with him?

You can establish your trustworthiness by:

- ♥ Being a personal witness to your product's reliability.
- ♥ Having experience and training.
- ♥ Building a solid track record of telling the truth.
- ♥ Having good will toward the customer that overrides any personal interest.
- ♥ Believing in what you sell.

Customers will trust you when they believe you're promoting *their* best interests rather than yours. You build trust by being honest and candid about the product. Honesty means you're willing to praise a competitor's product if you believe it's deserved. Customers want to hear you express any concerns about the suitability of the product for them.

They must believe that, if you don't carry the products and services that meet their needs, you'll support their buying from a competitor. At the same time, they should believe that you have such confidence in the value *you* offer that you would be shocked if they bought somewhere else!

Your *claims* about products will become credible when they are:

- ♥ Efficient to present, simply stated, easy to grasp.
- ♥ Coherent, logical, and well-reasoned.
- ♥ Consistent with other things the customer knows and believe
- ♥ Balanced among all aspects of the subject—the bad and the good.
- ♥ You show no bias for or against any product.
- ♥ Complete, touching all key issues.
- ♥ Interesting and vivid.

In other words, customers are most likely to trust you and feel loyal to you when you fulfill their "Ten Demandments," as articulated by Kelly Mooney:

1. Earn my trust.
2. Make it easy.
3. Put me in charge.
4. Play fair.
5. Inspire me.
6. Listen to me.
7. Over-deliver.
8. Stay with me.
9. Get to know me.
10. Remember me.[17]

The combination of the 4 E's brings you closest to fulfilling all ten of those demands. (We'll discuss these traits more fully in Chapters 8 and 9.)

Where to Start Building Your Trustworthiness

You build your trustworthiness from the inside. I learned this from my wife more than anyone else.

As you read about the hallmarks of trust, ask yourself, "How trustworthy am I?" By answering honestly, you have the best chance to shore up weak areas. Compare yourself with the following hallmarks of trust:

- ♥ I say what I feel in ways that show my respect for others' thoughts and values.
- ♥ I work to understand other people's concerns and issues.
- ♥ I don't raise my defenses when someone judges me.
- ♥ I acknowledge and apologize for my mistakes.
- ♥ I keep my promises.
- ♥ I am loyal to people, whether they are present or not.
- ♥ I make clear my expectations concerning others.
- ♥ I maintain confidences regarding personal and sensitive information.

Trustworthiness is hard-earned...and easily lost. It resides tenuously in a customer's mind. She'll drop it at the first sign of your deceiving her or breaking a promise.

Only after much testing does trust become hardy and forgiving. Once trust binds people together, they will extend themselves to support one another. My wife is a superlative example of that.

Signs That You Are Not *Credible*

A customer will give no credibility to a salesperson who:

- ♥ Has a bad character (dishonest, immoral, deceitful, hyper-critical, etc.). The customer will reason this way, "If this salesperson's a *bad* person, I can't trust what he or she says. I need to be wary."

- ♥ Is a hypocrite—the salesperson's own beliefs stand at odds with his or her claims and actions.
- ♥ Is biased—has a *vested* interest in distorting the outcome. "I think this salesperson wants to enrich him or herself, not help me. This salesperson's not being impartial."

Watch out for fallacies in your claims:

- ♥ Inexactness of language.
- ♥ Equivocation—using the same word to convey different meanings.
- ♥ Ambiguity—when the listener can't be sure which of a set of possible meanings is the intended meaning.
- ♥ Vagueness—using a term or concept that is indeterminate.
- ♥ "Heaps" and "slippery slopes"—using patterns in which boundaries or dividing lines are treated as if they were nonexistent.
- ♥ Leaving holes in your argument.

Chapter 7

Changing Your Mindset About Selling

"It's not the will to win that counts,
but the will to prepare to win that counts!"

—Paul W. "Bear" Bryant (1913-1983),
longtime coach of University of Alabama's Crimson Tide[18]

In almost every company, salespeople follow the same pattern—a few out-sell the rest by substantial numbers. It's the Pareto Principle: 20 percent of the sales force normally produces 80 percent of the results, while the other 80 percent drags in the remaining 20 percent.[19] I believe peak performers excel because of what they *do*—and what "average" salespeople are unwillingly to do.

Success leaves clues, so most average salespeople know what they *should* do, even *could* do, but *don't* do. I believe their not-doing is often due to fear or laziness: fear of asking for orders, prospecting for referrals, soliciting customers' names and addresses, making cold calls, and following up with customers who don't buy. Successful salespeople do these things consistently.

How they handle fear is one characteristic that separates the most productive 20 percent from the less productive 80 percent. I understand this because I was once in that 80 percent (fearful) group before I found ways to join the 20 percent (successful) group. I was afraid of rejection, of customers not liking me, of being too pushy. I was every customer's friend, but when it came time to ask for the sale, I froze up. You could say I had the Heart, but not the Mind for selling.

Fearing rejection, we often decide not to go through such situations. Yet in sales, we know that if we don't ask, we don't get the order. "Ask" is the most powerful verb in the selling world. It is also the essential ingredient in the Mind part of Heart & Mind Selling. Salespeople with a lot of Heart, or empathy, for their customers, and not enough Mind, or ego-drive, have the most difficult time asking for the sale. They lack the internal drive—the need to win—to push through fears and objections to close the sale.

So, how do you go from being afraid of asking for the sale to having the courage to persist until the end?

Turn Up Your Tension Thermostat

The key to acting calm in the face of fear is managing the tension in your mind. "Tension" is the power that motivates us to take risks. R. H. Grant said, "A salesman, like the storage battery in your car, is constantly discharging energy. Unless he is recharged at frequent intervals, he soon runs dry. This is one of the greatest responsibilities of sales leadership."[20] One of your essential jobs is managing your productivity so you *don't* run dry, and you can do that by turning up your mental "tension" thermostat!

You know the difference between a thermometer and a thermostat, right? A thermometer only reports the temperature; a thermostat has the potential to affect it. Thermostats regulate the heating/cooling system and make automatic adjustments to create the right environment. They monitor whether it's too hot or too cold and respond to correct it.

As a salesperson, your job is to set the thermostat to the correct balance so you feel productive, not paralyzed. As I'm writing this, it's a chilly winter weekend in Georgia. My home thermostat is operating to keep me warm. However, if the window next to me were open, cranking up the heat would be a waste. I must manage and maintain my environment for the thermostat to do its job.

Likewise, sales success is not just a matter of *increasing* tension in your life. You can increase productivity in your "heating system" by closing open windows that sap the heat. Plan your actions so that everything you do promotes the success you seek. Search for heat loss caused by the drafty windows of poor preparation. Align your actions with your goals and eliminate wasted effort. Set your thermostat tension to motivate and challenge you.

This "creative tension" I want you to develop is *not* a synonym for "stress." Stress is a negative, nonproductive condition of anxiety and strain. When we live under pressure from stress for an extended period, the stress cripples, even paralyzes us. People who operate under that kind of stress are constantly on edge—defending and preserving themselves, taking no risks, protecting their emotions, dissipating their energy. People in stress crises eventually stop caring and shut down.

Factors that trigger stress are everywhere. Unpredictable challenges produce tension: price increases, lagging sales, job restructuring, new technology, new procedures, tight money, challenging goals. Whenever gaps exist between what people want and what they really have, they react with either productive tension or debilitating stress.

By contrast, the creative tension I'm talking about *generates* productive energy. For example, the tension that actors produce while preparing to go on stage generates an edge that heightens their performance.

We have the power to *choose* either tension or stress. We can take advantage of our challenges and grow, or we can fear them and withdraw. We can't always shape our circumstances, but we can shape our responses to them by adjusting our thermostat.

Three Steps toward ACTion

When your vision of what you *want* is more powerful than what you *fear*, you create a desire that moves you to action! The formula is found in the acronym **ACT**:

1. Accept your current reality (your fear).
2. Create a vision of what you want (the benefit of action).
3. Take action (feel the fear and act on it anyway).

First, **Accept** your current reality. Tell yourself the whole truth about where you are right now and accept your feelings and fears. What are your weaknesses? What *aren't* you doing that peak performers *are* doing? Why? What would you like to do differently? What would you like to do less? What would you like to change or fix? Write these down.

Then, **Create** a vision of what you want. When you fix your reality, what will it look like? Create a picture of the state you want to achieve. Fill in details relative to what you will produce at work, how you will act with customers and managers, what you will provide for your family, how you will feel inside—whatever you want.

Just contemplating the gap between where you are and where you want to be can generate productive tension. Our subconscious tends to view this tension in one of two ways:

1. We change and uplift our current reality, moving toward our new vision,

   or

2. We debase our new vision, bringing it down to the level of our current reality.

Civil Rights activist Reverend Martin Luther King, Jr. knew the power of creative tension. In the 1950s and '60s, he worked to instill his dream in others. He wanted to build a positive tension that would uplift Americans and move them toward a new vision. In his 1963 *Letter from Birmingham Jail*, he wrote:

> Just as Socrates felt that it was necessary to create a tension in the mind so that individuals could rise from the bondage of myths and half-truths to the unfettered realm of creative analysis and objective appraisal, we must see the need...to create the kind of tension in society that will help men rise from the dark depths of prejudice and racism to the majestic heights of understanding and brotherhood.

Business author Peter Senge of the MIT Sloan School of Management summarizes the power of a vision in his book, *The Fifth Discipline*, by explaining creative tension. Senge says this creative tension is generated when we can plainly envisage where we want to reach—our vision—and at the same time, honestly discern where we currently are. He states that the distance between these two places creates a natural tension; thus, if we are lacking vision, there is no creative tension.

In *The Fifth Discipline*, Senge explains that creative tension cannot be created through one's analysis of their current situation because analysis alone cannot produce a vision. The misunderstanding of this is often the cause of the failure of people who are qualified to lead. "What they never grasp is that the natural energy for changing reality comes from holding a picture of what might be that is more important to people than what is," said Senge.[21]

By turning up your tension thermostat, you pull a spring of tension until it strains to be released. Because you're *pulling* yourself, you don't have to *push* yourself so much. Energy for change flows naturally out of your discontent in reality. People crave to achieve their vision when what they want to create is juxtaposed with their current state.

Let's look at it this way: If your boss told you several people were being laid off because the company was facing financial hardships, you might be worried. If he said your job was safe, you would relax. Then, if he said you would have to take a cut in pay, you might start looking for a new job on your own or find a way to patch the hole in your budget. You would respond to that tension. If you can create that degree of motivation on your own without a looming emergency, you're sure to move ahead!

The outcome of **A** and **C** is **T**: Take action. Peter Drucker said, "You can either take action, or you can hang back and hope for a miracle. Miracles are great, but they are so unpredictable!"[22] Action cures many situations, while analysis only regresses them.

Former First Lady Eleanor Roosevelt wrote, "You gain strength, courage, and confidence by every experience in which you really stop to look fear in the face…You must do the thing which you think you can't do."[23]

When you set your tension thermostat at optimal levels, you will more easily overcome fear or nervousness and be able to chart your progress with accuracy.

Now Is a Good Time to Create a Personal Scorecard

Now that you've identified what you want and turned up your tension thermostat, it's a good time to create a personal scorecard. Why? Well, how much fun is it to go bowling or play basketball without a tally? Keeping score lends meaning to the game. Even people who aren't competitive want to know how they are doing. The human spirit has a psychological need to grow and improve. We look anxiously for our grades after we've completed a class. We continually compare ourselves to each other or to our latest performance. I always look forward to reading the evaluations of the sales seminars I conduct.

Coach Pat Riley took an average NBA team, the New York Knicks, to the NBA finals in 1994 by simply setting goals and measuring something that most teams don't. Typical basketball teams measure rebounds, blocked shots, assists, points, and attempts. Riley measured hustle. He did this by assessing the number of rebounds the players went after and didn't get. He noted the number of times a player would dive for a loose ball, the number of times a player would stand in place to take a charge, and the number of times a player swatted at a ball and tried to steal it.

He didn't preach about hustle; all he did was post the results on a scorecard in the locker room at the end of the game. The players took notice. An ordinary team became a peak-performing team.

Most humans are at their happiest when they are striving, stretching, and lengthening their stride. The U.S. Army caters to this need when it claims that you can join the Army and "be all you can be." I know of no way to recapture opportunity that has been wasted in your past, but that's no reason not to seize every opportunity in your future. An African proverb says, "The best time to plant a tree is twenty years ago. The next best time is now."

Show yourself that you have the right stuff and be able to prove it with your scorecard. The higher your score, the more confident and skilled you will become…and the higher your sales will soar.

Start By Setting Goals

Start tracking your progress today. Honestly evaluate where you are, then set achievable goals for where you want to be.

What is a goal? It's a desire, an expectation, a target, a place you want to go, something you want to be. It's not something you want to *have*. We don't really work to *have*; we work to *be*, to *do*. You might say, "I want to have money." I think what you really want is to *spend* money and/or to save it for emergencies. You might say, "I want to have a new car." I think what you really want is to *drive* that new car. Having all the money in the world, or having the greatest car you can find, won't do you much good if you can't use it. Your future is not so much where you stand as in what direction you're moving. Goals determine where you'll end up!

Even if you're an old hand at setting goals, it never hurts to be reminded of the characteristics that goals must have in order to work. They must be:

1. **Self-ordained.** It has to be your goal; it can't be somebody else's. If it's not your goal, you're wasting your time. If you adopt someone else's goal, work hard for it, and finally reach it, you might find that you never wanted to be there in the first place, and you'll end up more discouraged than ever. You can increase your productivity by as much as 50 percent, and reach your goal faster, just by knowing exactly what you want. Don't be like a kid who goes to college for his parents, graduates, and becomes a beach bum!

2. **Attainable.** There is an old saying, 'if you want to eat an elephant, you have to do it one bite at a time.' If you set a goal you

can't possibly reach, you're setting yourself up for failure. And guess what? You'll fail. You can't possibly read *War and Peace* after dinner tonight or lose twenty pounds tomorrow. If you made $30,000 this year, it's unlikely you could reach a goal of $70,000 for next year. Set a goal that's attainable.

3. **Challenging.** At the same time, encourage yourself to stretch. If you made $30,000 this year, don't set a goal to make $30,000 again next year. Set your goal to make $35,000 or $40,000 or whatever you think you can really achieve. If you set a goal to *maintain* the same salary, you'll deflate your spirit of challenge and part of your productivity will die. A goal should be within your reach, but not within your grasp. Everything worthwhile has to be worked for.

4. **Measurable.** Set your goal in measurable terms. Use dollars, percentages, dates, numbers, etc. You can't attain goals like *I want to be happier* or *I want peace of mind* or *I want to be rich.* Those are worthwhile objectives, but they aren't goals. As you work toward your goals, you'll sense that you are gaining more of those objectives. Achieving a goal moves you toward your larger objectives. Without a goal, you may lose some of those objectives. Success is measured not by what you end up with, but by your accomplishment of getting, one step at a time, from where you are to where you want to be. If your goals aren't measurable and specific, you'll never know where you are on your trip from here to there.

It would be like your favorite football team going out to play another team with no scoreboard. They play, but nobody tells them the score until the game's over. That would be impossible. How would they know when to put out that extra spurt of energy? How would they know when to hold back? How would they know when to fight harder? How would they know whether to kick the extra point or go for two?

5. **Shared.** Achieving your goal will likely affect other people, so involve those who are connected to the goal's achievement in its formation. If it's a family goal, bring the whole family together to work out the steps. If it's a career goal, it will affect the company as well as your loved ones. If it affects no one but you, share it with a friend. Sharing your goal reinforces it, makes it easier to achieve, and helps secure your commitment to it.

6. **Written.** This is a key factor. Writing your goals helps you remember where you're going and gives you a specific road map to follow if you get lost. It's like the story of the brilliant accountant who studied a small piece of paper every morning before he started to work. Then he would lock it up in his desk drawer. Everyone was quite curious. One day, he left the drawer unlocked and his assistant found the note. It said, "Credits on the left, debits on the right." You see, sometimes we forget even the most basic things unless we write them down. Writing reinforces the goal in your subconscious.

7. **Restricted by time.** This means simply that a goal must have a deadline. The deadline presses you to reach the intermediate goals that will enable you to achieve your big goals. Otherwise, you'll just keep right on meaning to, and meaning to, and meaning to. If you're still waiting for "someday," I have a bulletin for you: Someday is always the day after tomorrow.

8. **Focused.** Make the goal narrow enough to allow you to see it at one glance. Have you ever seen professional golfers? They stand on the green and look and wiggle and look some more. Bowlers

do it too—they stand at the alley and look. Where are they looking? Not at the club or the ball. They're looking at the hole and the pins. That's the target point, their goal. Their goal is self-ordained, attainable, challenging, measurable, and shared. They've worked hard to get to this point. All that's left now is concentrating and focusing—blocking out distractions.

To begin selecting your goals, start with the end in mind and work backwards. Picture what you want and define the purpose, the need, and the objective you desire. Then devise ways to buy that car, build that machine, outline that new method of management, formulate that new operation, double those sales. Find ways to *reach* the goal you start for.

The Power of Keeping Score

"When performance is measured, performance improves," as stated by Thomas S. Monson,[24] is a sound leadership and self-improvement principle. I believe it was W. Edwards Deming who said, "If you can measure it, you can improve it. If it can't be measured, forget it."[25] Measuring, or keeping score, is a tool that creates change, and it may be the most powerful "hammer" you have for building success.

Keeping score *creates* focus, which helps us see what we want. Since we tend to move toward the focus of our attention, keeping score also prevents us from being distracted by all the little things that life throws at us.

What should we measure? Johann Wolfgang von Goethe, German writer and philosopher, aptly suggested, "The things that matter most must never be at the mercy of the things that matter least." Therefore, I recommend you focus on the things that most dramatically affect *results*. The Pareto Principle asserts that a minority of causes or efforts usually leads to a majority of results.[26] Applied to selling, this principle has one theme: Measure for the most crucial results you can produce with the least expenditure of time, effort, and assets. The way to assure that you do the things today that will *produce* those results tomorrow is to make that personal scorecard we talked about.

Rarely are those who produce dramatic results lucky. They produce results because they focus on the things that *cause* them. In retail sales, the factors that dramatically affect results are closing rates, average sales per ticket, and credit sales. These are the statistics I would include on my scorecard.

Can you encourage your customers to help measure progress for your scorecard? How about taking the initiative to call them, or at least send them a survey form? Ask how the product looks, and how they feel about it now that they've used it. Find a way to encourage them to respond after installation. (Sears®, Old Navy®, and the Olive Garden®, for example, offer a $5 discount off the customer's next purchase in return for answering a satisfaction survey on the telephone. You could do that.)

You can observe customer satisfaction with internal operating statistics. You can track customers who don't buy and evaluate why. Imagine the information you could learn by knowing why your customers buy or don't buy! If creating customer allegiance is the most important foundation for ongoing business growth, and their loyalty is the way to make sure you reach your own personal goals, then it's foolish to think that no news is good news, and that you should let sleeping dogs lie. The truth is: No news is *bad* news.

And be sure to share your information within the company to stimulate others to improve performance.

Never underestimate the power of keeping score. Creative tension and keeping score cause a salesperson to take action. Action is the key characteristic of Mind. Measure, measure, measure. Baseball teams do it, basketball teams do it, hockey teams do it, football teams do it. So do Heart & Mind salespeople.

Part III.

Tools for Building the Heart & Mind Connection

In this section, you will learn how to measure the degree of Heart you bring to every sales transaction, how to determine your unique Selling Personality as well as the unique Buying Personality of every customer, how to better understand your customer so you can create a Heart & Mind connection, and advanced techniques for building Rapport.

Chapter  8

What's Your Selling Personality?

"To thine own self be true."

—William Shakespeare

You're a nice enough person. You go out of your way to love and serve your customers. But this one customer is really giving you a hard time. She seemed really interested in your product or service when she called, but when you start talking about features and what makes it unique from the competition (the same speech you always use!), you notice her eyes start to gloss over. She yawns. You start to sweat because you can just feel in your bones that you're blowing the sale. What should you say? Is it already too late?

You get into the office to find an email in your inbox entitled URGENT. It's from one of your best customers. Apparently, her last order never arrived, and now she's taking the heat from one of her clients. The tone of her email is nasty—almost personal. How will you handle the situation?

Will you call the customer right away and calmly listen while she tears your head off? Ignore the email and let her anger pass? Reply to the email outlining clear goals for how you will rectify the situation? Talk to other people in your office—maybe your manager—to get insights on how to solve the problem?

You've got one week to put together a very important presentation for a very big client. Are you more likely to start writing the entire presentation now to get it over with, write a little bit every day, work on it obsessively the entire week up until the final hour, wait until the day before to write it, or just wing it and hope for the best?

What's Going On Here?

In each of the situations described above, you are faced with a problem. How you act is determined by who you are and how you see the world; in other words, your personality or your behavioral style.

Each of us has a unique behavioral style—no two personality styles are alike. That makes sense when you consider the millions of variables that shape and define who we are and why we are the way we are. You grew up in a two-parent house; maybe one of your peers grew up with just a dad. You were raised to be religious; he was raised to believe only in himself. You had a family who was willing to support your way through college; he had to work nights just to pay tuition. These are just a few examples of the many variables that make us so different.

But despite the many differences, researchers and scientists have un-covered similarities in behavior and personality styles that bind groups of people together. Though you and your friend may not share the same personality style exactly, you have enough in common that you can be grouped together in the same basic category. Not surprisingly, people who belong in the same category get along together much better than people who belong in differing categories.

Just as you have your own unique behavioral style that defines how you act in certain situations, you have a unique selling style as well. Think of it as your sales personality. This doesn't mean you always act the same way in every situation; it simply means that you have a common set of behaviors and ways of dealing with customers and situations you tend to fall back on when you're not conscious of what you're doing. Consider it your comfort zone or your default setting.

Your customer also has a unique personality and therefore a unique style for making purchasing decisions—a buying behavioral style. Again, this doesn't mean your customer always buys one way. You may catch her on days when she's making decisions that seem totally out of character. It simply means that your customer has a tendency to act one way when faced with making the decision to buy.

Do you think that knowing what a customer's buying behavioral style is gives you a tremendous advantage in every selling situation? You bet. It matters more than you think!

The Importance of Rapport

Have you ever met someone you just didn't like? He seemed like a nice enough person, but something about him just got under your skin? Of course. It happens all the time. So what do you do? You deal with the person when you have to but otherwise keep your distance. You act civilized and treat him politely, but you don't go above and beyond to become his friend.

What if your customer feels this way about you? Wouldn't this affect your ability to close a sale? How about establishing customer loyalty? Wouldn't this prevent you from being able to build the Heart connection we've been talking about so far?

One of the fundamental truths about selling is that customers only buy from people they like and trust. In sales jargon, we call this rapport, which is a French word that signifies a relationship of mutual respect and love between two people. Another term to describe it is compatibility. We seek compatibility and rapport in every situation and we see its effects everyday. We like people who are just like us—who share the same personality style—and we tend to get annoyed and frustrated with people who aren't.

What happens when we interact and communicate with people who aren't like us or don't have the same style? The opposite of rapport happens: friction. Friction in a sales situation is disastrous, both for the short-term goal of closing the sale and ultimately when it comes to building the lifetime relationship. The deadly thing about friction is that it is so silent. Your customer isn't going to tell you how annoying or abrasive you're being, and unless you can read her body language, you will keep on creating friction until it's too late. You might even close the sale—we've all bought things from salespeople we didn't like. We felt pressured or too embarrassed to say no. The difference is we never went back!

The opening scenario to this chapter gives you a perfect example of what happens when you and your customer don't share the same personality style. You've got this interested customer and this really great product or service to sell. In your mind, you're saying exactly what you need to say to close your sale, but to your customer, you're just going on and on about something she just doesn't care about. You're selling using your expertise and knowledge, but she's interested in how others perceive her when she uses the service and product (a true sign of an Enthusiasm buyer). She's looking to buy from someone willing to flatter her ego. And like two ships passing in the night, you go your way and she goes hers—never really knowing what came between you.

The rule is very simple. Customers like salespeople who are just like them. In other words, they feel comfortable buying from a salesperson with a selling style that matches their buying style. Since you can't screen the customers who walk through the door, you'll do well to understand and know how to adapt to all styles. I call them the 4 E's:

- ♥ **Empathy**
- ♥ **Ego-Drive**
- ♥ **Enthusiasm**
- ♥ **Expertise**

When you become skilled at selling to each buying style, you will be able to tailor your sales strategy to each customer who walks through the door. You'll eliminate friction and create rapport. But before we take it that far, what about you? What's your selling style? What's your dominant approach towards the world?

Your Pace and Priority

To understand Pace and Priority, we must first explore personality styles. You are probably familiar with personality tests. If you haven't taken one, you've at least heard about them. In these tests you are forced to answer questions about your attitudes and preferences with only a limited number of choices. Some assessments contain only a dozen or so questions, while others ask hundreds. The choices you make identify patterns in your behavior, which are called personality traits. These identify your specific personality style.

No one is truly just one personality type, of course. We each have a blend of factors, and we adapt our behaviors to fit certain circumstances. Some assessments reveal both our "basic wiring" and where we go when we're under pressure.

The basis of our personality (and selling) style is Pace and Priority. This explanation isn't supposed to slap labels on people or put them in boxes. Of course, people are more complicated than these factors alone, but so much information becomes available to you when you can identify these two characteristics.

Pace

Everyone has a preferred operating pace. Some of us prefer a faster pace, while others operate at a slower pace. Except when we consciously alter it, we tend to follow our natural pace.

Faster-paced people react more quickly to their environment. They walk faster, talk faster, eat faster, make decisions faster. Their lives are filled with places to go, things to do, people to meet. They tend to be more outgoing and less reserved. They are extroverts and seem to have a lot of things happening at once. If they were a car, they would be speeding. In fact, many seem to have only an accelerator—and no brakes. Their operative word is GO!

Slower-paced people take their time in responding to their environment. They walk slower, talk slower, eat slower, make decisions slower. Their priority is *not* being in motion all the time. They tend to be more reserved and less demonstrative in their interactions. They are introverts and prefer to concentrate their energies on doing fewer things. If they were a car, they would be under the speed limit. They use their brakes frequently and don't push limits. Their operative word is WAIT!

It's important to understand that one pace isn't better than the other. One's not right and the other wrong, although there are times when one pace can be more appropriate than the other. For instance, at a traffic light, all drivers agree that green means go and red means stop. But slower-paced people think yellow means stop because the light is turning red; faster-paced people think yellow means hurry so they can maintain their pace and move traffic along.

What's your pace—is it fast or slow?

Priority

Which is more important to you: completing tasks or having stronger relationships? When you work on a project with others, do you emphasize completing the project well and on time, or do you focus on helping others do their jobs and feel valued? Some call these characteristics Happening and Harmony.

Again, one priority is not better than the other, although one might work better at certain times.

If your priority is getting *things* done, you tend to focus on achieving results or following processes. People may seem like a distraction, so you put people's needs second until the task is finished. Because you push for completion, others may see you as uncaring and cool (if not cold) toward others. They may consider you a high-tech person because *things* may interest you more than *people*. You're Happening, not Harmony.

On the other hand, if you prioritize *people*, you focus more on relating to them. You're willing to compromise projects and deadlines if necessary for people's needs. You may feel that tasks are only a means to help people. You don't let the task distract you from what really counts: people! As a result, others probably see you as warm. You are a high-touch individual, because your number one priority is involving yourself with others. You do better on the welcoming committee than on the planning committee. You're Harmony, not Happening.

Which do you prefer—people or tasks?

Four Quadrants

By overlapping the two circles in the previous illustrations, we create four quadrants in which people tend to be primarily:

- Faster-paced and task-oriented
- Faster-paced and people-oriented
- Slower-paced and people-oriented
- Slower-paced and task-oriented

Which combination best describes you? Your answer will tell you which of the 4 E's is your dominant style. As you read on, remember that none of these preferences is right or wrong, good or bad—they are just different. Knowing what drives your preferences, choices, and behaviors is the first important step to building rapport

Faster + Tasks

If you enjoy working at a faster pace and completing tasks, your dominant style is **Ego-Drive**. You like to be in charge. Your motto could be: "Lead, follow, or get out of the way!" You are energized by change and challenges, and you're not afraid of a little conflict. You say what you think and expect others to do so as well. You want bottom line results and you prefer bullet points to detailed explanations. You are a goal-setter and driven to get whatever you go after.

You don't like to be given orders—having options and making your own choices is important to you. Usually you operate as an individual, not as part of the herd. You take risks and press ahead when others step back. You seem less interested in "making right decisions," because you have a strong will and can work hard to "make your decisions right." You tend to emphasize results, provide direction, utilize power, and bring direction. The Heart of salesmanship may not come easily to you.

As a Selling Style

Ego-Drive is the desire to work to produce a result. In selling, you desire to make a sale. Ego-Drive generates a sense of urgency, a goal-oriented approach, and a "fire in the belly." Ego-Drive salespeople need a result—to win or to achieve or to serve others or to feed their families. Whatever the reason, they are driven.

To achieve a result, they'll risk rejection, failure, and loss. They know what they want; moreover, they believe they are worth it. They sell more when they can use sales tools that are familiar to them. Most peak performers are naturally Ego-Driven, and they add the three other traits.

Ego-Strength is a crucial ingredient of Ego-Drive. It gives you resilience to bounce back from rejection and increase your motivation for the next try. When you lose a sale, Ego-Strength will prevent you from feeling devastated. It allows you to believe in yourself, your products, and your company strongly enough to stay on course in spite of setbacks

The motives behind Ego-Drive can vary. A few Ego-Drive salespeople are *self*-centered. They have fallen into *egotism*—an out of control pride that seeks to dominate the customer *and* the selling process. Often, they can connect only at a "transaction" or "let's trade" level—if you do this for me, I'll do that for you. A trade, however, as fair as it may be, builds no loyalty to you or your company. In my experience, *other*-centered Ego-Drive yields more sales and long-term relationships. I guarantee that you can succeed as a professional by influencing others for *their* good.

Faster + People

If your drive is to operate at a faster pace but your compass steers you more toward people, your dominant style is **Enthusiasm**. You tend to be highly sociable. Your motto could be: "There are no strangers, just friends I haven't met!" You measure your success in terms of popularity, approval, and acceptance. You tend to be more emotional than logical, and you probably have difficulty managing your time and making deadlines because you overestimate your ability and underestimate your commitments. If conflict affects approval, you can be political, but you use charm (rather than force) to get things accomplished. Too much detail is distracting to you, and you tend to act on impulse. You trust people easily if you can relate to them. You see yourself as a team player, perhaps even their cheerleader. You tend to emphasize participation, provide enthusiasm, employ emotion, and bring inspiration. The Heart of salesmanship should be a snap for you—if you take the time.

As a Selling Style

Enthusiasm is a spirited, intense, and excited feeling and a motivating and mobilizing inner drive to think, act, and feel in a concerted way to reach a goal. The goal can be to promote a cause or another person.

A salesperson's unfeigned Enthusiasm is contagious. The positive emotions you radiate tend to override any opposing emotions in the customer, such as skepticism or worry. As a result, the customer aligns her feelings with yours.

Slower + People

If you need a slower pace and are people-oriented, your dominant style is **Empathy**. You tend to be steady and sensitive to the needs of others. Your motto could be: "No one cares how much you know until they know how much you care." Appreciation is important to you, and you tend to go out of your way to help others. You conceal your emotions and try not to make a fuss if you disagree, because you dislike conflict and being the center of attention. You may agree to a proposal you are against in order to keep the peace. Long-term loyalty, ongoing assistance, and teamwork are very important. You dislike surprises and like to specialize and complete one project at a time. You are a support player, not a star, and prefer operating behind the scenes. You tend to emphasize inclusion, provide stability, utilize sincerity, and bring harmony. The Heart of salesmanship may already be part of your selling process.

As a Selling Style

You may recall that several studies consider Empathy the number one quality of top salespeople. As you may recall, Empathy involves considering other people's viewpoints and truly understanding them. When you have Empathy, you appreciate the other person's perspective and include it with your own considerations and calculations. It's the core component of Heart & Mind Selling.

Empathy salespeople want to listen to and befriend the customer in order to find a solution that fits her needs. Salespeople with Empathy are not pushy; they don't force a close. Empathy produces the best sales results when combined with the other three styles. If you are strong in Empathy and weaker in the other three styles, you can succeed by adding aspects of them to your Empathy.

Slower + Tasks

If you need to operate at a slower pace and concentrate on tasks, your dominant style is **Expertise**. You tend to be accurate and precise. Your motto could be: "Measure twice, cut once!" Planning and caution are very meaningful to you. You tend to operate by reason, making lists and balance sheets to accomplish your goals. Timeliness and efficiency hold high value, and others who share such tendencies impress you. You get along best with people who are like you. You follow processes to reach a desired result and are neither an innovator nor a pioneer. You use facts and data to win arguments and have little patience for estimates, emotionalism, or ego displays. You tend to overanalyze, and you want to know outcomes before you begin. You can come across as skeptical and untrusting because you ask difficult questions. You emphasize accuracy, provide analysis, utilize logic, and bring objectivity. The Heart of salesmanship may not come readily to you because of its emotional and time involvement.

As a Selling Style

Expertise salespeople rely less on showmanship and more on objective data. They expect the facts to speak for themselves. They are more "tellers" than "sellers." I've heard it said that people who know *how* work for people who know *why.* Expertise involves both how *and* why. It includes:

- ♥ Your knowledge of the industry and its products and your particular store and its products and services
- ♥ Your skills in providing solutions

For the Expertise-oriented salesperson, your capacity and predilection for product facts and figures can be both a strength and a struggle: a *strength* because you know so many details and can discuss them; a struggle because too much detail can annoy customers with other buying styles. After you've learned so much about a product's features and benefits, it's tempting to want to share it all. Enthusiasm can easily overwhelm a consumer. Too much product information can cause other styles to tune you out. It creates cognitive dissonance or confusion. If a customer becomes confused, she will be unable to make a decision.

Expertise-driven salespeople often rely so much on logic and information that they sterilize their environment and kill the passion that brings customers into their store in the first place. Remember we said that people who know *how* work for people who know *why*? It's a *why,* not a *how,* that brings people into your showroom, but Expertise tends to emphasize the *how*.

Knowing *how* works for customers who already know *why* when they walk in. They're counting on you to supply them with a *how* that will make their *why* happen. So you don't need to help them find *why*. However, you do need to support it, even build a larger fire underneath it. Be careful, though, as you explain *how* that you don't douse their fire by telling them too much.

Chapter 9

Finessing the 4 E's to Create Ultimate Rapport

"The better your relationships, the shorter your sales cycle, and the more money you will make."

—Dan Brent Burt, *Selling the IBM Way*[27]

Which style have you identified as your favorite selling mode? It's important to know, because it's the hammer you will most likely use to drive your message home to customers—once you become familiar with these new tools.

Have you figured out that most of us *sell* in the same style we like to *buy*? As a result, it's easy to sell to similar-style customers and harder with others. If you could, would you choose the easy way and cherry-pick only those with your style? Well, even if you probably could cherry-pick, think of the potential sales you would lose. You will succeed to the extent that you expand your selling style to accommodate all consumers. You decide how many you want.

Since I've found it both necessary and worthwhile to be compatible with every customer, I'm encouraging you to *commit* to learn all the buying styles. Learn to finesse them, so you can skillfully handle yourself in the customer's comfort zones. When you become adept at applying all four attributes—Ego-Drive, Enthusiasm, Empathy, and Expertise—you'll be able to *romance* more people more often. As Goethe wrote, "We must always change, renew, rejuvenate ourselves; otherwise we harden."

Which natural buying style keeps you upbeat? If your style is Enthusiasm, you need to particularly concentrate on growing Expertise. Likewise, if Expertise is your strength, work on your Enthusiasm. If your style tends toward Ego-Drive, learn to employ Empathy. If Empathy is your forte, beef up your Ego-Drive motivations. You need a blend of all four to be your best.

I'm not saying you have to *become* another style, or pretend to be something you're not. Instead, you'll just be developing new skills and learning to finesse the styles not naturally yours. Finessing new styles is like adjusting the water for a shower—you're simply mixing hot and cold.

By some unknown law, the balance of hot and cold water in the shower is never the same as you left it—even if you were the last one to use it. You must put your hand under the water and adjust until the temperature is right. You're OK until someone flushes a toilet and turns the water hotter. Then you adjust for more cold water. When someone turns on hot water, the shower turns chilly, so you turn the handle back toward the warm side, blending the two styles again. Using others' buying styles is similar; you just adjust as consumers change the situation.

Now, remember how it feels when you finally get the temperature right? You step in and *a-h-h-h*! Wonderful, soothing perfection. You want to stay with that feeling for a long time. That's the way it is with our customers when we finesse, blend, turn up the most comfortable style for them, and turn down the least comfortable one—they will want to stay with us for a long time.

Finessing Empathy with Ego-Drive

Taken alone, Empathy and Ego-Drive oppose each other. Empathy works to match one person's understanding with another's, while Ego-Drive works to change the other person's understanding. What both characteristics have in common is initiative. People with both traits don't just think about acting—they *act.*

A healthy perspective sees Ego-Drive and Empathy as the two ends of a see-saw—neither moves much if one significantly outweighs the other. But when balanced, they work together to make you a successful salesperson, even as they seem to work against each other. Ego-Drive is the motivator that launches you toward your potential customer. Empathy is the insight that guides you through your customer's evasions and objections. Empathy and Ego-Drive complete each other.

Both your Empathy and Ego-Drive should be motivated by selflessness. Empathy should discover how customers think and feel, so you can help them select a solution that promotes their interests. Ego-Drive without Empathy is often employed for selfish ends, influencing the customer for the seller's self-interest. Such motivation produces short-term sales, but no hope of a customer for life. When an Ego-Drive seller is motivated to satisfy the *customer's* interest, the salesperson believes the customer's investment will serve them both. That sincere belief makes the process of influencing the customer a natural service without selfish pushing at all!

With a strong Ego-Drive but insufficient Empathy, you'll tend to close sales through sheer determination. However, you may lose the sale if the customer throws you a curveball. You'll disqualify yourself as a solutions provider if you can't meet her needs or objections. You'll only land the ones who can't stand up to your forceful will. Lots of Ego-Drive with little or no Empathy creates a "what's in it for me" attitude. These salespeople assert their own interests. They talk and promise too much, listen and deliver too little, and neglect to call customers after the sale. They are pushy and aggressive and ultimately drive the customer away.

An Ego-Drive salesperson can become more effective by incorporating some of the Empathy characteristics and behaviors:

- ♥ Develop more patience.
- ♥ Tone down your directness and ask more questions.
- ♥ Work on your body language to be more approachable.
- ♥ Offer more encouragement in conversation.
- ♥ Let others control more of the decision-making process.
- ♥ Be more enthusiastic and persuasive.
- ♥ Build the customer's ego and self-esteem.
- ♥ Stress benefits.

On the other hand, a salesperson with ample Empathy may fear to assert his Expertise. For example, more often than not, sales presentations end without the customer being asked for the order. Few salespeople ask for the customer's name and address on the first visit. Few ask for customer referrals after the sale. When customers raise objections, many salespeople quit selling and just pass out their business card. Average salespeople earn average (mediocre) wages, and an average Ego-Drive is part of the problem.

A great deal of Empathy without much Ego-Drive creates a "nice guy" image. But his very niceness prevents him from closing sales. He acts as if it's more important that people *like* him than *buy* from him. While Empathy produces friendships, it doesn't put braces on your kids' teeth or groceries in your refrigerator. The dentist and the grocer prefer cash to kindness. Solid sales success requires *both* Ego-Drive and Empathy. Finessing these characteristics will help you find the balance for long-term stability.

An Empathy salesperson can be more effective by developing some of the Ego-Drive characteristics:

- ♥ Be more assertive and direct.
- ♥ Cope better with change.
- ♥ Get less involved in the emotional reasons for the sale.
- ♥ Make communication brief and to the point.
- ♥ Stick to the topic.
- ♥ Eliminate time-wasters.
- ♥ Be more in charge and decisive when appropriate.

A salesperson lacking in both Empathy *and* Ego-Drive is an order-taker, a clerk who cares little for the customer, and may care even less about making the sale.

A salesperson who possesses both traits, and can blend them appropriately as each customer requires, may recognize the paradox: Make sales with Ego-Drive even as you find and serve the customer's interests with Empathy. Empathy is critical for cementing relationships in trust. Ego-Drive is crucial for solving the issue and closing the sale.

Are you flexible or rigid? People who study animal behaviors say that it's not always the strongest of a species that survives, nor the most intelligent, but the one that's most responsive to change, the one that bends easily. In humans, it's the one who appreciates and employs the control that comes with choice.

If Ego-Drive is your dominant buying/selling style, you know exactly what I'm talking about. You want to study all the options before you decide on anything, because you're motivated by results, not intentions. You pursue predetermined outcomes and are seldom deterred by challenges and obstacles.

Regardless of their personal preferences, however, all salespeople must understand how important both choice and control are to those who buy in an Ego-Drive mode. For this style, "take-away" techniques can be very effective. Suggesting that a buyer may lack the resources to acquire a particular product and should consider a lower-price, lower-quality alternative often has the effect of cementing her decision to get the best. Such a strategy is not generally as effective with buyers motivated by Enthusiasm, Empathy, or Expertise. But being in control and making confident choices is a big motivator for Ego-Drive buyers. Learn to value, and use, this "hot button" appropriately.

Peak performers, applying both Ego-Drive and Empathy in appropriate amounts, promote only solutions that fit *that* customer. It is the Heart & Mind combination. They can push (and never quit), but their customers don't feel pushed, because they know your heart desires *their* best interests. Be aware, however, that these two forces rarely work in *equal* amounts. Some customers need more support, while others need more pushing. Finessing the two will help you balance the scales.

Finessing Enthusiasm and Expertise

Can you see how Enthusiasm and Expertise can be another see-saw combination? Enthusiasm expresses feelings, intuitions, and attitudes. Expertise deals with facts, logic, and efficiency. Enthusiasm tends to be about emotion and fun; Expertise tends to be about reason and business.

At an upscale steakhouse, servers may make a *show* of delivering sizzling cuts of meat to a diner's table. They call this "selling the sizzle." The "sizzle" sells the steak to nearby patrons more effectively than any written description on a menu. That's the Enthusiasm part of the equation. The customer's emotional experience with the dinner is at least as important as its culinary quality.

At the same time, Expertise is prevalent in the menu description before you order the "sizzle." The Health Department's inspection rating is another measure of Expertise! Diners value both Enthusiasm and Expertise, and a restaurant can't stay in business without either one. Neither can a retail outlet.

Telling you to apply both Enthusiasm and Expertise to serve each customer may sound complicated and exhausting. Actually, it's quite simple. If you are naturally Enthusiastic, develop some behaviors of Expertise:

- Listen more carefully.
- Become more organized.
- Be more logical and systematic.
- Provide more details.
- Create more follow-through.
- Be more careful and quiet.
- Be more factual and systematic.

For the same reason, Expertise salespeople will do well to develop some behaviors of Enthusiasm:

- Approach customers more informally.
- Be relaxed, sociable, friendly, and supportive.
- Focus on communication.
- Let customers verbalize their thoughts and feelings.
- Be more open.
- Accept differences and learn about all products.

- ♥ Never answer unasked questions.
- ♥ Tell customers only what they need to know to make decisions.
- ♥ Show personal acceptance of others' choices.

It's About Perfection!

We humans, despite our delusions, don't work rationally, but emotionally. As Carl Rogers, author of *On Becoming a Person*, said, "The curious paradox is that when I accept myself just as I am, then I can change."[28]

We *can* adjust our selling style when we accept ourselves. And we *must* adjust or we'll lose our customers. Don't think of your style as superior to others. No one style is all good or all bad. Styles describe, not prescribe, how we act. They just *are*. They are one of the paradoxes of our lives. Our goal should be to finesse our paradoxes, not to eliminate them. Don't expect the customer to adapt to your selling style. Plan to adapt your style to your customer's.

I'm challenging you to consider the information in this book on the 4 E's and the related selling and buying styles to see how you can employ your distinctive differences to *complete* rather than *compete*. To become perfect! In the first century BC, Horace, a Roman philosopher, observed, "The very difficulty of a problem evokes abilities or talents which would otherwise, in happy times, never emerge to shine." He must have known that you would be struggling, many centuries later, with the paradoxes of selling, and wanted you to know that mastering these skills will be worth the effort.

You'll gain rapport and have greater influence with customers as you gain ability to finesse the paradoxes. The contrasting selling styles within you can dovetail nicely to bring about peak performance. Creative friction between the styles can produce a greater result. I'm suggesting that you receive these apparent contradictions gladly.

Although it's certainly easier to stay in our natural selling styles, and many people have come to reject certain behaviors as being "too hard," "too wild," "too passive," or "too bold," remaining static may deny you the rewards that come with learning to be more like others—and the sales that come with it!

We'll come back to the 4 E's throughout the book. In the next chapter, we'll see how selling styles and buying styles correlate—or don't.

Chapter 10

What's Their Buying Personality?

"Seek first to understand, then to be understood."

—Stephen Covey,
The Seven Habits of Highly Effective People[29]

Several years ago, a car dealership put its sales staff through six hours of intense training in behavioral selling. In the weeks following, the team eclipsed its long-standing records for daily, weekly, and monthly results. The general manager said, "We no longer sell cars. Instead, we make customers happy!" Ultimately, this is the business of all selling professionals: to make customers happy. Happy customers will return to buy again, and will recommend us to friends.

In another car dealership, a salesperson who was familiar with personality styles watched as a couple entered the showroom. They walked slowly, which he took as a clue to how they would prefer to be approached. He noticed that the man went first to the dealer invoice sticker on the window of a certain model. He wrote notes and paid attention to details. This was a clue that the husband was in a task-oriented mode.

The woman was more interested in the car's interior. She seemed to be visualizing where each family member might sit. The salesman concluded she was people-oriented. With this information in hand, he approached them in an unhurried, unexcited manner, giving them space and asking how he could serve them. He planned to present with Expertise to the gentleman and Empathy to the lady. They told him they had already resolved to purchase another brand of car and were driving to that dealership. They decided to stop here for a last due-diligence comparison.

The salesman said he knew the car they had settled on was good, and asked for permission to provide data and dependability information on the model they were looking at in his showroom. His tone was reassuring and calm; he demonstrated that he respected their ability to decide. He eliminated hyperbole while showing great confidence in the style, quality, and value of his vehicle.

The couple spent enough time to satisfy their questions, thanked him, and headed toward the door. Then he asked, "Do you already have a sales associate you're meeting at the other dealership?" When they said no, he recommended they ask for John, who would be happy to take care of them.

In John's sales kit were only some Enthusiasm tools and a few Ego-Drive tools. He hadn't received personality style training and only knew how to sell *his* way. He came on too strong—balloons and hot dogs for the kids they didn't bring along. He sold too quickly—a special deal if they acted right away. He answered questions they hadn't asked, and told them details they didn't want to know.

They left without buying the vehicle they had earlier decided to buy. Three days later, the couple returned to the first dealership to re-examine the car they hadn't seriously considered. They then bought it from the salesman who sold according to their buying styles.

Get Out of Your Bubble!

Customers—people—see the universe as *they* are, not as *others* are; they look at the world through eyes colored by their own behavioral style. They are much happier being in a world (or a store) of people who already think like them. They don't need to change to fit someone else's version of truth. Thus, when the customer sees a likeness in your selling style and her buying style, she loses any reason to feel threatened.

When customers meet a salesperson with a conflicting style, they feel like saying, "You just don't understand." Has anyone ever said that to you?

If we could all take a moment to see the other person in a different mirror, perhaps it would be a better world for us all. Every customer is different. All you have to do is discover her needs.

With this idea in mind, let's look at customers' four basic buying styles. Just as you have a dominant selling style—whether it is Empathy, Ego-Drive, Enthusiasm, or Expertise—your customers have similar defaults for buying. How can you tell what that style is?

Begin by observing the customer. Your first impression of her is as important as her first impression of you. When you *first* see her, notice:

- ❤ What is the customer wearing?
- ❤ What is the customer's pace—fast or slow? What other visible clues does the customer provide about her pace?
- ❤ What is the customer's priority—task- or people-oriented,

happening or harmony?

- ♥ Is the customer carrying anything—an ad, notebook, color swatches?
- ♥ Does the customer have children with her?
- ♥ Are there two adults? If so, which is the customer?

Your observations serve as a scouting report. What clues did you observe that could indicate her personality style and likely buying style? The key elements to look for are how fast or slow the customer moves and talks and whether or not she's open or closed in her relations with you. Is the customer talkative or shy? Process the information quickly and use it to help you develop your approach.

Modify your initial approach to match the customer's style, so you can extend your influence and effectiveness from the beginning. Caution: When you classify customers, you don't want to *force* them into category boxes, or slap labels on them. No one is all one way or the other. Most people operate somewhere between the extremes. Moreover, their pace and priorities vary in different settings. People are more complicated than these factors alone.

That said, you can apply the 4 E's to learn useful information about customers. Their style reveals their "basic wiring," which is their comfort zone. You can expect them to feel pressure or stress if you invite them to step out of it.

Empathy Buyers

Empathy buyers tend to fit a slower-paced, people-oriented profile. They don't like to be pressured or pushed around. Nothing turns them off more than the salesperson who leads with, "Find something you're interested in?" They're focused on taking their time and making the right decisions. They'll depend heavily on your careful guidance and wisdom. They may flip-flop a few times before they make a firm decision. You know you have Empathy-driven customers when you see them pick up a product, read the back, put it down, walk away, and come back five minutes to repeat the whole cycle again. Sometimes, they just can't pull the trigger!

Empathy buyers are driven by relationships. They expect a warm and friendly greeting and they're usually okay with being touched. A gentle pat on the back, a firm handshake, and plenty of eye contact are great ways to earn their trust and solidify the relationship. Because they are driven by relationships, they may ask for time to talk a decision over with their spouse or friend. They generally keep a small circle of acquaintances and family members they count on for guidance and direction. One thing you don't want to do with an Empathy-driven customer is insult her decision-making process. Salespeople often shoot themselves in the foot with these types of customers by insisting that they don't need a spouse or friend to help with the decision, but *they do*. If a customer does bring a friend or family member with her, don't cut them out of the conversation. Solicit their feedback as well. Empathy buyers will appreciate this.

Empathy-driven customers resist change whenever possible and hate conflict. Sometimes this can be frustrating because it requires you to slow down your pace and stand by as the customer plays through hundred "what if" scenarios in her head. It can also be hard to get direction and feedback from her. If a customer doesn't like your product, she may not tell you out of fear of hurting your feelings. You might spend a lot of time going down the wrong direction only to have to backtrack and start over. Empathy-driven customers may feel more comfortable with disappearing from the scene than dealing with conflict, so do your best to encourage honesty and openness from the very beginning of the relationship. We've all had customers we thought we serviced well, but disappeared and never came back. Many times these are Empathy buyers who can't deal with having to tell you they were actually unsatisfied.

Empathy-driven customers may need some hand-holding, but once you've built the relationship with them, they're generally customers for life.

They are looking for *tradition*:
- ♥ Slow deciders who want friendship.
- ♥ Family-oriented and possibly shy.
- ♥ Prefer "known" to "new."
- ♥ Don't like change.

How to identify them:
- ♥ Desire to learn more about you.
- ♥ Indecisiveness.
- ♥ An amiable personality; niceness.

Your best approach to buyer:
- ♥ Pace your approach and take it easy.
- ♥ Provide statistics and demonstrate reliability.
- ♥ Be relationship-driven.
- ♥ Motivate with friendship and trust, not deadlines or insistence.
- ♥ Outline what to expect.
- ♥ No surprises.

To create a receptive environment:
- ♥ Chat about family and personal life.
- ♥ Provide sincere responses.
- ♥ Answer their questions with simple examples.
- ♥ Ask what their concerns are.
- ♥ Empathize with their desire to serve others well.

Typical questions in their minds:
- ♥ Why should I switch now?
- ♥ What if it doesn't work for me?

- ♥ What is this product's or store's track record or history?
- ♥ Is this all I need, or are there add-ons?
- ♥ How good is the warranty?
- ♥ My current supplier gives good service—why should I change?
- ♥ Is it difficult to switch over, and is there assistance?

Ego-Drive Buyer

Ego-Drive buyers tend to fit a faster-paced, task-oriented profile. Your biggest problem with them is boring them to death. They want everything fast and they want you to cut to the chase. They approach everything with one question in mind: "What's in it for me?" Answer that question—fast—and you'll have them in the palm of your hand.

Ego-Drive buyers are driven by results. Unlike Empathy buyers, they don't want to build a relationship with you. They prefer getting down to business. Cut the chitchat about the family, the kids, and the dog—just give them the facts (in bullet points) they need to make the decision. But not too many. Ego-Drive buyers don't like too much technical information—it only slows things down. They like having options, so you can make their life easier (and yours) by listing their options one by one and explaining the pros and cons of each decision. They think in numbered lists and bullet points. Be warned: They will know when you haven't done your homework, so prepare. Ego-Drive buyers will ask you a lot of questions and they will come at you fast. You'll build trust with them by being able to answer them quickly and by demonstrating your confidence in your answers. Always make an Ego-Drive buyer feel in control.

Ego-Drive buyers have difficulty with trust. They operate from the position that salespeople are trying to con them or pull a fast one, so they won't tolerate aggressive behavior. A couple of years ago, a salesperson friend of mine was dealing with a very difficult Ego-Drive buyer. The Ego-Drive buyer had his mind set on a very specific product. The salesperson led the gentleman to the product and then tried to suggest to the customer some other similar products he might be interested in. The customer told the salesperson to "stop harassing him" and stormed off. All the other customers in the store stood and stared, which left the salesperson feeling a little red in the face.

Ego-Drive buyers are "take charge" types of people. They're the CEOs of the world. Think Donald Trump and Martha Stewart. They're motivated by risk and being ahead of the curve, which makes them easy to convince. Unlike Empathy buyers, they'll be more open to trying new things and changing their old habits, just as long as you can clearly define the benefits of doing so in 15 seconds or less.

They are looking for *innovation*:
- ♥ Quick deciders with strong ego.
- ♥ Multitasking entrepreneurs.
- ♥ Appreciate innovative design.
- ♥ Welcome new changes.
- ♥ Fear of being "played."

How to identify them:
- ♥ Bossy.
- ♥ Honest.
- ♥ Direct.
- ♥ Stepping on your words.
- ♥ Short attention span.
- ♥ Talk loud; talk fast.

Your best approach to buyer:
- ♥ Make them feel that they are in control.
- ♥ Get down to business.
- ♥ Provide direct answers.

- ♥ Acknowledge their accomplishments.
- ♥ Ask for their feedback and opinion.
- ♥ Motivate with testimonials, data, or details, not hugs.
- ♥ Never use force or manipulation.

To create a receptive environment:
- ♥ Emphasize challenge, rewards, and results.
- ♥ Present the high points and the bottom line.
- ♥ Provide services that take care of the details.
- ♥ Recognize that they are solution-driven.

Typical questions in their minds:
- ♥ What does it cost?
- ♥ When can I get it?
- ♥ Is this the latest version?
- ♥ Is this your best model?
- ♥ Can I change or upgrade it?
- ♥ Do you really believe what you're telling me?
- ♥ How will this free me for more important pursuits?

Enthusiasm Buyers

Enthusiasm buyers have a faster-paced, people-oriented profile. They're social creatures who will talk your ear off for 15 minutes before letting you speak. They're warm, affectionate, and highly likeable people. You will know you're dealing with an Enthusiasm buyer when you feel yourself open up and relax. They'll have you laughing at a joke, most commonly about themselves.

For Enthusiasm buyers, the focus is on recognition. Their purchasing decisions usually revolve around how a product or service will increase their status or make them stand out. They're most likely to buy something because a celebrity endorses or uses it. They like to be the first ones among their friends to discover the next hot trend, so they're open to innovation and new ideas and products. If you can get them hooked, they'll likely spread the word among their friends. They're the original Buzz Marketers.

Enthusiasm buyers aren't shallow, but they care about image. They may judge you on the way you look or how you carry yourself. Do you wear Armani suits or the $99 special from the bargain basement down the street? Everything is about the show with these types of customers; they will gravitate to products or services that allow them create or communicate to others the perception that they are successful. They're like the real estate agent who rents a BMW® on days when she meets with new clients or does an open house just because it communicates that she's a winner. "Perception is reality" is their motto.

Though Enthusiasm buyers like to move fast, they want the sales process to be fun and easy. They prefer to discuss business over dinner, or drinks, or even a game of golf. Like Ego-Drive buyers, they don't like to be bogged down by boring details. They hate paperwork and they hate reading. You can help your Enthusiasm buyer by narrowing down the options. However, they don't respond to aggression or conflict. If you come on too strong, they will perceive you as being less interested in them and more interested in closing the sale. Enthusiasm buyers are friendly and fun, but they expect to be the star. When dealing with them, stroke their ego.

They are looking for *show*:
- ♥ Impulsive deciders who want approval.
- ♥ Socializers and storytellers.
- ♥ Want to try things out.

How to identify them:
- ♥ Lots of smiles and laughing; expressive.

- ❤ Talk with their hands.
- ❤ They may reach out and touch you first.

Your best approach to buyer:
- ❤ Present energetically to make the best impression.
- ❤ Provide personalized follow-up and service.
- ❤ Be emotion-driven.
- ❤ Motivate with endorsement, not details.

To create a receptive environment:
- ❤ Recognize their efforts.
- ❤ Provide time for socializing.
- ❤ Bring them back to the topic by using their own words.
- ❤ Ask how they feel about ideas.
- ❤ Summarize and connect important points.

Typical questions in their minds:
- ❤ What's in it for me to buy this?
- ❤ How will buying this make me look good?
- ❤ Will I enjoy this, or will it be more work and responsibility?
- ❤ Is there flexibility in the price?
- ❤ Is there a payment plan?
- ❤ Who else is buying this product?
- ❤ Can we discuss this over coffee?

Expertise Buyers

Expertise buyers tend to fit a slower-paced, task-oriented profile. They are the engineers, lawyers, accountants, and software developers of the world. They're highly methodical in their thinking, preferring to focus on one problem at a time. If you try to move them to the next step too fast, they will fight back. Expertise buyers work at their own internal pace. Like Empathy buyers, they fear making the wrong decision, so give them plenty of information and then step back and let their brains go to work. They'll eventually get where you want them to be; it'll just take some time. Their motto is: "Slow and steady wins the race."

Expertise buyers value knowledge and information. With them, there's no such thing as too much information. Give them charts, graphs, any piece of marketing material you have. Many times, they'll have information already with them. They never go into anything blind. Expertise buyers are process people. They are highly rational and practical people. They care about the bottom line benefit, but they're sometimes more interested by how something works. If you were selling them a sneaker, you wouldn't emphasize style so much as its state-of-the art features, the technology that makes it the best product on the market.

Expertise buyers are low risk people. They look both ways before crossing their kitchen floor and they're the type of people who pack seven pairs of underwear for a three-day trip. You'll do best with these customers by eliminating the risk. Emphasize the money back guarantee, the warranty, the 24-hour customer service—anything to ease their minds. Because Expertise buyers tend to be rational, hard facts people, don't be insulted if they don't warm up to your jokes or humor. They're not cold fish; they're just uncomfortable dealing with strangers. It may take the first few times of dealing with you before they muster up the courage to look you in the eye. You would do them a favor by eliminating the awkwardness of the selling situation. Keep your conversations short. Don't ask them too many personal questions. Direct your attention on the merits of the product and the service.

Above all, Expertise buyers want to be considered smart. After all, they already think they are. Make them feel like they made the one intelligent, logical purchase out of the many options out there, and they will come back to see you again.

They are looking for *provens*:
- Cautious deciders who want details.
- Value-oriented and suspicious.
- Look for inaccurate statements.
- Need to know how things work.
- Like to be admired for their intelligence.
- Avoid conflict and debate.

How to identify them:
- Very rational.
- Shy.
- Talk...real...slow.
- Ask intelligent questions.
- Dress plain; all tucked in.

Your best approach to buyer:
- Present proof, results, and background.
- Provide rational, unemotional testimonials.
- Be quality-conscious.
- Motivate with facts, not concepts or ideas.

To create a receptive environment:
- Avoid chatter and emotionalism.
- Provide a detailed package.
- Be understated in your comments and opinions.
- Ask them to decide for themselves.
- Itemize the benefits of deciding soon.

Typical questions in their minds:
- Is this a proven product or a new idea?
- What is your warranty?
- How does this product compare to others?

- ❤ How are your people qualified?
- ❤ How long has your company been in business?
- ❤ Will this product match my exacting specifications?

Chapter 11

Putting it In Practice

"Tact is the ability to describe others as they see themselves."

—Abraham Lincoln

In 1979, Lee Iacocca took over as president of Chrysler® Corporation and convinced Congress to guarantee a $1.5 billion loan from banks to rescue his number three auto company from bankruptcy. At the time, it was very controversial. It could have set a precedent for more government bailouts.

Everything was riding on how the "new" Chrysler® would appeal to prospective customers. Some serious reframing of Chrysler in consumers' minds was in order, because the American public thought about Chryslers as they thought about Ramblers—not often and not well. Or not at all. Just four years later, the company emerged from bankruptcy and was able to pay back all its loans. How did Chrysler rebuild its brand?

Iacocca and his marketing team made a big impression in 1980 by using a daring Ego-Drive approach. Standing in front of a shiny black "power car," dressed in a "power suit," Iacocca jabbed his index finger into the camera and told viewers, "If you can find a better-made American car, buy it!"

They chose this tactic because first adopters of new technology and innovative products tend to be Ego-Drive buyers. This type responds to challenges and is more willing to take risks. The Chrysler campaign produced widespread buzz, and the company backed up its promises with performance.

The next adopters of new products tend to be Enthusiasm buyers. Chrysler® introduced *new* vehicles and re-popularized convertibles as a way to reach those customers' desire for fun.

In addition, they created the minivan for family-oriented Empathy buyers. Then, when they had established a record for building reliable vehicles, they began touting an extended quality warranty, which appeals best to Expertise buyers. Next, they enlarged their market by buying Jeep®. (Later, Chrysler was bought by Mercedes-Benz®.)

Chrysler sold more vehicles. Of course, it didn't win over every prospective buyer. But, without that customer-style plan, I doubt that Chrysler would have survived.

I'm not suggesting that your first approach to a customer should be based on Ego-Drive. That approach may not work where consumers don't consider your retail market to be high-tech or innovative. Floor coverings, for instance, are well established in our culture and don't need a planned *introduction* in the marketplace. Instead, they need a planned, finessed *connection* to each customer. **The secret is not which style you sell in— it's being in the same style as your buyer!**

Besides trying to sell in the customer's buying style, remember to blend *each* of the selling styles into *every* customer interaction. No one has only one buying style. Start with the style that the customer seems to prefer. However, as you proceed, add elements from the other three styles while you emphasize the prospect's preferred approach. Doing so will ensure that you'll communicate more effectively. Great salespeople *romance* their customers so they feel *loved*! If you want to sell consistently, you really have no other choice!

As you commit to becoming the best salesperson you can, remember: The best salespeople have the ability to finesse the paradoxes of influence.

If Empathy Isn't Your First Impulse

Some personality styles find it difficult to express Empathy effectively. Even when you truly understand another's situation, if you can't communicate that understanding, it doesn't count.

Empathy springs from accepting these five facts of life:

1. Other people count as much as I do.
2. Others' viewpoints deserve consideration.
3. Others' feelings and beliefs are as valid to them as mine are to me.
4. The better another person and I understand each other, the more likely we can work together comfortably and contribute to each other's success.
5. The more people feel understood, the more open to influence they become.

Empathy is not the same as sympathy. It's similar, in that sympathy feels with the other person. Unlike Empathy, however, sympathy adopts the other's feelings. Sympathetic salespeople won't push the sale if the customer offers excuses, even when the product is the right solution. Instead, sympathy feels sorrow or pity. Sympathy lets people off the hook rather than solving their problems.

Successful salespeople know the difference between Empathy and sympathy. They recognize that they don't have to *agree* with the customer's perspective to understand it and accept the person. Before presenting a product, they work to uncover all sides of issues—the customer's, their own, and any others that seem useful. That's Empathy. But it must be genuine. If you don't really care, most customers quickly realize you're a phony.

In my experience great salespeople are honest, assertive, persistent, and non-threatening. A well-known sales trainer has said if the customer tells you you're a good salesperson, you most likely are not. What the customer really means is that he feels he is being sold something he would never buy on his own accord.

You may eventually wear down a customer and force a sale, but she won't be pleased about it. And she won't be happy to see you on the next visit, *if* she returns at all. Furthermore, she's far more likely to develop buyer's remorse when she gets the product home.

The highest praise a salesperson can receive from a customer is that he makes sense. Salespeople can evoke this reaction through empathy. When the salesperson uses empathy, the customer does not feel like he is being sold, but that he is fulfilling his needs. However it is often up to the salesperson to help the customer realize he *has* those needs. It is a widely held belief that customers are much more likely to buy more from someone who seems to make sense than from someone they view to be a great salesperson.

Empathy and compassion connect us through a shared language of feelings and experience, one heart to the next. How often do you invite a customer to trade up to luxury because you know it's what she really wants? How many times a day do you say something like, "Can you imagine how beautiful your room will look with this new recliner and those accessories?" How well is your showroom staged to resonate with your customers' emotions?

When you *genuinely* empathize with and care about a customer, your chief motive is providing her with the most fitting solution. You would pass up a sale rather than sell against her best interests! Genuine Empathy relieves any differences of perception between you and your customer, and builds trust, which engenders her lifelong loyalty.

Paul Tournier, the Swiss psychiatrist and medical missionary, wrote, "He who loves, understands; he who understands, loves. One who feels understood, feels loved; and one who feels loved, feels sure of being understood."[30] If you struggle to feel Empathy, don't let its importance escape you. Learn to master this skill. With emotion alone, you're only a cheerleader. Without Empathy, you offer no *romance*.

If Ego-Drive Isn't Your Strong Suit

Ego-Drive is a little more complicated. At first, it doesn't seem to follow the rule that salespeople should adopt the same style as the buyer. Imagine what would happen if a high Ego-Drive salesperson attempted to sell to a high Ego-Drive customer. What should be a pleasant experience for both parties would turn into a battle of wills! The salesperson and the customer would be too busy competing with each other to develop any kind of connection—let alone a Heart & Mind one. As we've discussed previously, you need to nurture an Ego-Drive that is *other*-directed. Now the rule makes sense: A salesperson selling to an Ego-Drive buyer (often a *self*-directed one) should adopt an *other*-directed Ego-Drive selling style.

The easiest way to strengthen your *other*-directed Ego-Drive is to build your Expertise, Enthusiasm, and Empathy. When you do, you will naturally feel driven to benefit others with what you know and have.

Using Ego-Drive may feel unnatural at first. If so, recall a time in your life when you became the cheerleader for some product, cause, or person. You felt excitement about the product's value and how it had helped you! Do you remember the Ego-Drive that impelled you to tell others about it because you wanted to help them attain the same benefits you enjoyed?

If It's a Stretch to Feel Enthusiasm

Everyone can feel Enthusiasm, but some show more of it more often than others. Enthusiasm works on different levels, has different causes, and appears in different forms. Some people feel *energized* by people and events. They love to call a friend and talk for hours. Others feel weakened by people. They prefer the inner world of ideas or working alone, such as solving a crossword puzzle. Some people are determined to balance their checkbooks to the penny, while others round off to the nearest ten dollars. When you understand these differences, you can shape your job to give you more energizing tasks and fewer de-energizing tasks.

Try this exercise: List your job responsibilities. Rate your enthusiasm for each on a scale of **1** (lowest) to **10** (highest).

  ____ Helping customers
  ____ Completing paperwork
  ____ Attending sales training meetings
  ____ Dealing with difficult customers
  ____ Reading brochures about new products
  ____ Straightening up the sales floor

_____ Presenting benefits to customers
_____ Researching
_____ Answering questions

For each low-Enthusiasm task (your rating of 1-5), ask yourself, "Which part of it don't I like?" (We often like *some* parts of a job that we don't enjoy as a whole.)

Say, for example, you don't like presenting benefits to customers. Try to figure out exactly what aspect of the task you don't enjoy. Is it the difficulty of remembering all the benefits? Do you have trouble understanding them? Is it the challenge of persuading the customer?

Then ask yourself, "Why don't I like it?" Is it because you think more about why *you* want them to buy the product and less about why *they* should want to buy it? Or some other reason?

What could you do to make the task more appealing to you? How might you change your attitude to give you a little jolt of Enthusiasm? Here are some ideas:

- ♥ Practice until you can do the task efficiently and effectively.
- ♥ Learn to turn yourself on. Remember a time you were excited. That excitement is contagious and communicates that you believe in your product. You convey your conviction.
- ♥ Learn more. If you resent dealing with certain customers, read articles about dealing with difficult people. Think of every customer as your best friend or grandmother. How would you work with their quirks? Then practice on a few new prospects.
- ♥ Ask co-workers. If, for example, you don't like paperwork, ask the person who whistles while filling out forms why he likes pushing a pencil.

If You're Not Inclined toward Expertise

Salespeople without a natural preference for Expertise may find it especially challenging to become an expert. If that's you, you're likely tempted to rely on your natural selling style. Remember these words of caution: You may lose sales if you can't use all four attributes. Customers' trust doesn't flow only from your showing Empathy; their confidence doesn't spring only from your Ego-Drive; their friendship doesn't come only from your Enthusiasm. Your product knowledge enriches those results. No matter which natural style you're blending it with, Expertise raises the customer's confidence in you, opens the door to trust, and leads the way toward friendship.

While you may not need to become a *certified* expert in your field, you do need to master the basics so you know more than the average consumer. When you're confident of your Expertise, you don't hesitate when a customer asks for your professional input or personal opinion. Your self-esteem shouldn't rest on whether customers *accept* your advice. Rather, measure how well you offer a clear, objective, sensible perspective that helps them make their buying decisions. Buying decisions are *their* responsibility and choice to make. When your customer perceives you as an expert, trust is automatically increased.

Learn to Be Flexible

In my seminars, I show the Yin and Yang symbol in front of the paradoxes listed above. When I ask what it means, some reply "life and death." It actually refers to the balance and harmony between life's apparent opposites. Conflict is always at work in life—it's natural. One truth doesn't negate another if we see them in balance.

All of us experience the Yin and Yang principle in daily living. The challenge is to finesse opposition when the balance isn't equal. Some days, we have more Yin; some days, more Yang. Some days, more serenity; some days, more friction. All kinds of paradoxes and potential conflicts are inherent in our job of selling as we consider people and relationships, and as we see conflicting buying and selling styles, needs and wants, viewpoints and preferences.

The challenge is *managing* the paradox, not *eliminating* it.

Conflict and friction make life demanding, but they can be sources of beauty and wonder in our universe. According to NASA, shooting stars, those amazing streaks of light we see in the night sky, are caused by bits of dust and rock called meteoroids that encounter friction as they fall into our atmosphere and burn up.[31] Without friction, we wouldn't be able to see them. This same friction between a grain of sand and the lining of an oyster produces a pearl. Likewise, it's resistance to weight that builds muscle. As author Orison Swett Marden said, "Success is not measured by what you accomplish, but by the opposition you have encountered, and the courage with which you have maintained the struggle against overwhelming odds."[32]

As difficult as adjusting may sound, it will likely require just a 10 to 20 percent improvement from where you currently stand.

Over a hundred years ago, psychologist William James observed (an insight he says he gained from a carpenter) that "there is very little difference between one man and another, but what little there is is very important."[33]

Successful people are not unique because of one or two gigantic things they do 100 percent better than everyone else—they are successful because of the hundreds of things they do 1 percent better.

Chapter 12

Selling to Men vs. Women

"Women speak and hear a language of connection and intimacy, and men speak and hear a language of status and independence. Men communicate to obtain information, establish their status, and show independence. Women communicate to create relationships, encourage interaction, and exchange feelings."

—Judy Rosener, *America's Competitive Secret*[34]

The 4 E's are useful tools for understanding the Hearts of your customers. But customers are different in more ways than just personality. Understanding these differences and how to adapt to them is just as essential for building customer rapport as adapting your Ego-Drive selling style to match the Empathy buying style of a customer.

In this chapter, I'm going to explore a few of these differences and give you some additional techniques for overcoming them to build customer rapport. But a word of caution: There's always a danger in generalizing too much about what makes us different. That's why I advise you to consider this information about gender buying styles with the 4 E's. This will help give you a more complete picture and help you adapt to customers who don't play by all the gender rules.

The Rise of the Female Buyer

Who is the primary consumer of goods and services today and how does she choose a store? You have the first clue right there: Female dominance applies in most consumer retailing. According to Media-Mark Research, 90 percent of married women identified themselves as their household's principal shopper.[35] And according to *American Demographics* (as quoted in *The Atlanta Journal-Constitution*) women control 85 percent of the household income in the United States, which adds up to almost $3.5 trillion in annual spending.[36]

Even traditional male sectors, such as automotive, financial services, and technology, have made efforts to attract women consumers. More than a decade ago, for example, General Motors® rolled out the Saturn® model specifically for women buyers, making sure to hire female sales staff to sell the cars. Merrill Lynch®, Charles Schwab®, Fidelity®, and other financial services companies now market expressly to women, offering such lures as life-stage retirement advice and investing seminars. Even the pool table industry has learned the value of the WAF (Wife Acceptance Factor). According to Mark McCleary, vice president of marketing for Brunswick Billiards, their internal campaigns now carry the phrase "male initiated, female approved."[37]

Women buy 83 percent of all consumer purchases—including 94 percent of home furnishings, 80 percent of do-it-yourself products, 92 percent of vacations, 51 percent of consumer electronics, 60 percent of cars, and 91 percent of all houses.[38]

As business author Tom Peters writes in his treatise, *Everything You Need to Know About Strategy*, "Women's increasing power—leadership skills and purchasing power—is the strongest and most dynamic force at work in the American economy today...even bigger than the Internet."[39]

So what do your female customers *think* about you and your company? What do they *feel*? Why do they buy from you? How do they buy? How should a salesperson approach them?

I often think the average price for home improvement products would be higher if the industry were not run almost entirely by men. Picture a woman shopping in a floor covering store and sorting through a rack of samples. A well-meaning salesman approaches and offers some friendly advice. "I've got a cheaper one over here," he says as he motions to an assortment of budget items. "You don't need to spend that much."

Maybe *he* can't comprehend anyone spending that much, but *she* can. Chances are she has a deep emotional attachment to her home and understands the reasons to invest in premium floor covering. She believes that it's a sensible, practical way to add value to her home while at the same time enhancing the décor. For her, *quality* is a top priority. She should be that salesman's most prized customer. Instead, he points her toward the discount rack.

Is it because most flooring salespeople are men that Peters says women consider them to be only slightly better than used car salespeople?[40] Is that why up to 40 percent of customers who walk into a flooring store walk out and postpone the purchase?

Few people in the home improvement industry recognize that their core consumer does not view their products as a commodity. Women tend to understand that buying something for her *home* is not the time to pinch pennies. I saw this firsthand when my wife and I remodeled our kitchen. I was inclined to go with laminate countertops. They're adequate and nice. But my wife was set on the more costly granite countertops. Granite was the trend and she would be the first to admit that her kitchen is emotionally important to her. When we discussed the significant difference in price, I employed all my debating and communication skills, but we eventually installed granite counters. Once again, women buy all the stuff, and yes, the kitchen looks great.

In another personal retail shopping experience, we were looking at big screen TVs. The salesperson had articulated all the features and benefits of each model, and I had narrowed it down to two choices. I said to my wife, "Honey, I like this one. It has over 100 lines per square inch, so it has a better picture. Which do you like?"

She pointed at one on the other side of the display area and said, "I like that one. It has just enough room on top for me to put a plant or that new vase we bought in New York."

I'm a smart buyer, and so is my wife. We just buy for totally different reasons. My reasons are usually based on measurable facts; hers, on comfort, appearance, or functionality.

The big-box home centers like Home Depot® and Lowe's® are hustling to capture more of these anticipated female dollars. They are testing various retail formats to find out what works. They know their current strategies have to change in order for them to capture more market share. They also understand that the key is a better understanding of the female shopper, because they recognize a woman's increasing role as both a consumer and an influence on purchases.

Do you position your product to women as a *commodity* purchase or as a *value* purchase? Which is more common in your store: salespeople who understand and use the emotional words of decorating, color, and comfort; or salespeople who think their customers' shopping experience is like selecting a sack of potatoes? If the latter, it's a good bet that your margins will rise after you teach your salespeople to first consider female customers' emotional needs and their desire to buy products that offer a psychological lift. Get them to use a little Heart & Mind in their selling!

This is particularly true when customers trade up to luxury. Research from the Boston Consulting Group indicates that a growing number of America's middle-market female consumers are trading up.[41] Since the 1970s, the number of women in the paid labor force has increased by 112 percent—nearly 65 million in 2003.[42]

Nationwide, almost a third of working women now out-earn their husbands and 48 percent provide half or more of their family's income[43]—no wonder many feel justified spending a bit on themselves and their homes. These women happily pay a premium for goods and services they believe will deliver extra value in their quality, performance, and emotional engagement. Although the home is the leading category for trading up, value also rules in the office, in life—and in business.

Buying Differences between Men and Women

George Simons, co-author of *Transcultural Leadership: Empowering the Diverse Workforce*, believes that gender is the root paradigm of all human differences and constitutes our biggest social gap. In our culture, females are traditionally taught to put relationships ahead of winning, achieving, and "dealing."[44]

Males, on the other hand, learn how to be rivals early in life. They are expected to be aggressive, dominant, independent, and competitive. Parents may instill these differences or they may try to teach all their children alike. In various, subtle ways, however, the results are the same: starkly different styles of communication, building working relationships, and buying habits between the genders. Unfortunately, many salespeople don't recognize that such differences in buying styles are largely driven by gender.

According to Faith Popcorn in her book *Clicking: 17 Trends That Drive Your Business and Your Life*, the biggest gender difference is that men's genetic makeup prepares them to be strong protectors, while women excel as peacemakers. Men typically prefer to work side-by-side with other men with little verbal interaction. Women are nurturers by nature and prefer to make face-to-face contact, talking more frequently and more intensely. Men favor information over *romance* and emotion. They use "report talk" and focus on their independence and status. Women want *romance* and emotion rather than information and use of "rapport talk." They strive to maintain intimacy and create connections.[45]

Given how differently men and women are brought up, it's surprising that they can communicate with each other at all, especially when one is trying to persuade the other. Because we usually expect others to respond as we do, and often consider the other's differences to be "wrong," a transaction between a man and woman holds many opportunities for mistaken assumptions, frustration, hurt feelings—and lost sales.

According to anthropologists, man was the protector and hunter in earlier cultures. He was focused, always on a mission. His goal was to find his prey, kill it, and bring it home to feed his family. That's how today's man *shops*! He aims to achieve a result as efficiently as possible. Get in, find what he needs, and get out, hopefully without having to ask where something is. Men move faster and impatiently through a store's aisles to the section they want. They pick something up, examine its features, and are ready to buy.

Conversely, women from earlier cultures swept their eyes across a wide arc of vision so they could monitor any sneaking predators. Likewise, when today's woman *shops*, her sensors are going full bandwidth. She perceives everything: Is the parking lot clean, well-lit, and safe? How does the product look on the shelf? Are the store and its restrooms clean? Are the aisles wide and easy to navigate? Does the signage make the items easy to find? Is the salesperson dressed appropriately? How fitting is the product presentation?

She collects hints about how you operate, and she finds them everywhere: in the products you carry (*Do the products fit my desires for fashion and function?*), in your surroundings (*Do the sights, sounds, and smells please or upset me?*), and in the humans (*Do the employees want to work here? Do they want to help me? Do they use words I like? Does their body language invite me in?*).

Females also have a *hearing* advantage that contributes significantly to what's called "women's intuition." It enables women to "read between the lines," especially with salespeople. To your female customer, the sale is as much about how she feels about your personality or service attitude as it is about product facts. If the personal chemistry isn't right, she moves on.

All salespeople—men and women—should not appear too eager with female customers. Eagerness can destroy trust. We can't press or push. Our assertiveness must be tempered by our concern for the customer's needs. We must never talk down to her or use industry jargon she might not understand. Most of all, we should be patient while listening. Female customers especially want to feel that we would rather build a relationship than make the sale.

As Mary Lou Quinlan recommends in *Just Ask a Woman: Cracking the Code of What Women Want and How They Buy,* if you want to sell more to women, add "love" and *romance* to your marketing mix.[46]

I think all this boils down to the revelation that we need a fresh selling model. To communicate better and sell to the opposite gender more easily, men and women need attitude changes. You should be willing to acknowledge their differences and appreciate where each excels. Adopt some of the communication techniques of the opposite sex. Spend most of the time building a relationship, rather than trying to make a sale. At the same time, dial up the information and dial down the pressure. Ask more relevant questions, listen more carefully to discover the customer's real reasons for buying, and then personalize the benefits he or she will receive from the product.

Every conversation, of course, is more art than science. You carefully observe your listener's reactions and adjust accordingly. There are few selling strategies that will fail more quickly than being determined to talk in a particular way—your way—no matter what else happens. This is especially true when talking with the opposite sex.

Therefore, I urge you to apply this knowledge when you sell. **When selling to a woman, sell more like a woman buys; when selling to a man, sell more like a man buys.**

Selling to Women

[Before we begin the next two sections, I must note that these are very broad *generalizations*. Use these sections only as a general reference point, but remember that some people will behave indepdently of these tendencies.]

The typical woman shopper:

♥ Wants to be listened to intently.

- Wants salespeople to demonstrate that they heard what she said by acknowledging her verbally and nonverbally.
- Likes salespeople to ask questions, nod, make good eye contact, paraphrase, and reflect the feelings she has expressed. Salespeople should ask more, tell less.
- Appreciates salespeople who concur with what she says, rather than dispute, argue, or contradict.
- Wants salespeople to move through the process thoughtfully and in her sequence, particularly with expensive contracts.
- Would rather have time to establish trust and to buy at her own pace. Salespeople should avoid giving advice unless asked.
- May just want to look, and wants salespeople to respect that and give her space. Salespeople should not pressure or push for a decision.
- Is more open to general conversation.
- Wants to be taken seriously. Salespeople should introduce themselves and shake hands.
- Wants to be treated as a respected, valued, intelligent, financially-able consumer. Salespeople should never condescend.
- Responds well to salespeople who go slowly, earn her trust, and let her set the pace of the process. She wants to be thoroughly educated on the product or service. Salespeople should separate education from selling.
- Appreciates salespeople who keep in touch even after the sale is over.

Selling to Men

The typical male shopper:

- Rarely wants to be helped. He never asks for directions.
- Does not want to chit-chat. He wants to get down to business. Salespeople should be direct and specific.

- ♥ Views the sale as a transaction, a mission to be accomplished, or a problem to be solved. Salespeople should get to the bottom line.
- ♥ Goes *buying* not shopping.
- ♥ Needs to feel that salespeople are credible and know their product.
- ♥ Likes salespeople who act confidently.
- ♥ Responds well to salespeople who use money, business, and sports terminology.
- ♥ Appreciates salespeople who use humor and lighten up.
- ♥ Prefers salespeople who approach the situation more logically and decrease the emotional intensity.

Chapter 13

Another Quick Technique for Enhancing Rapport

"To effectively communicate, we must realize that we are all different in the way we perceive the world and use this understanding as a guide to our communications with others."

—Tony Robbins, author and motivational speaker

To build ultimate rapport, not only do you need to take into account the buying style (Ego-Drive, Enthusiasm, Empathy, or Expertise) and gender of your customer, you need to observe and match your customer's body language in the first few seconds of conversation. Matching nonverbals facilitates communication and builds connection. When two people blend naturally and subconsciously, they are in rapport. So it pays to mirror your customer from the outset. If she gestures often and seems to wear her feelings on her sleeve, feel free to be more demonstrative and open. If she conceals her feelings and acts more restrained, reflect that back. If she sits, you should sit. If she smiles, you smile. Again, your goal is to increase the sense of affinity and rapport.

Match her words, phrases, tempo, and voice level. Matching the customer's words and voice carries such power that experts study it. The science, called Neuro-linguistic Programming, focuses on listening to the words people say and responding in their style.[47]

Neuro-linguistic Programming identifies three styles of people:

 VISUAL PEOPLE connect to the world through visual images. They love to read, watch TV, and go to movies. When they think, they move their eyes up and to the left. Usually, they speak, think, and breathe rapidly. They describe happenings in terms of sight. They use phrases like "I see what you mean…That looks right to me…I need to get it into perspective…I get the picture…That's an enlightening answer…I'm in the dark about it…Watch your language."

 AUDITORY PEOPLE relate to the world in terms of sounds. They relate events to songs or musicals. They love music, the sound of a TV, and the background noise from a radio. They may hum or whistle unconsciously. They think with their eyes toward the left or by glancing from side to side. They have a moderate speaking rate, and breathe deeper and more evenly than Visual People. Many seem to listen to a different drummer. They use phrases like "That sounds right…That rings a bell…Suddenly it clicked…Just listen to me… I'm tuned into it…I hear what you're saying…Something tells me that's the answer…That's music to my ears…I can hear how serious you are."

 KINESTHETIC PEOPLE relate to the world through feelings and touching. They unconsciously (or consciously!) run their hands over products or touch them to their cheek. They feel products, squeeze melons in a grocery store to test freshness, pick up items from your desk, and brush away pet hairs. They like snuggling, pets, people, and babies. They speak and breathe slowly and deeply. They think with their eyes down and toward the left. They say things like "That feels right…It's an intense feeling…It's a smooth answer to a tough problem…Give me a concrete example…I'm groping for the right choice…I have a firm grip on the decision…I find it difficult to handle…I'll try to control myself."

A Final Word

You can use these strategies and rules to enhance your relational selling. When you build rapport with customers, you gain influence. Everyone wins because you apply the methods with integrity and honesty, and you help the customer make her best decisions.

Chapter 14

The 7 Universal Laws of Influence

"Thaw, with her gentle persuasion, is more powerful than Thor with his hammer. The one melts, the other breaks into pieces."

—Henry David Thoreau (1817-1862),
American author

If you've ever seen any of the *Star Wars*[48] movies, you know about "The Force." The Force is the hidden element or energy field that binds the entire universe together. It's kind of like gravity, except you can control it, harness it, and use it to move objects and people any way you want.

Yes, I know *Star Wars* is a movie, but there is a universal force equally as powerful in the real world that you can use to deepen your Heart connection with customers and direct their Minds towards making the sale—*Influence*.

Influence is neither physical force nor command. We call it "influence" only when the influencer *and* the one influenced *recognize* their alternatives and are free to choose. If the one influenced is *not* free, we call this power *coercion* or *manipulation*.

I have spent much of this book so far showing the ways in which customers are different and how you can adapt to these differences to create a Heart & Mind connection. But influence is something that applies to everyone. We are all equally affected by it, regardless of personality and gender differences.

In his landmark book *Influence: The Psychology of Persuasion,* Dr. Robert Cialdini equates influence to the instinctual behavior some animals demonstrate to physical stimuli they experience in nature.[49] His very famous example is that of the mother turkey, who will only care for its chick if it makes a "cheep-cheep" sound. If the chick doesn't make the sound, the mother will often kill it, believing it to be a predator. In experiments, scientists found that the mother turkey will care for anything—even a stuffed animal of a polecat, its natural predator!—just as long as there is a tape recording nearby playing the "cheep-cheep" noise of a baby turkey. Cialdini called the turkey's behavior in this situation a *ClickWhirr* response. The sound triggers a reaction, a *Click*, which causes the turkey to behave one way, a *Whirr*.

In his research of top salespeople, successful advertisers, and marketers, Cialdini found that humans act on the same *ClickWhirr* principle when making purchasing decisions, often without even knowing it.[50] The most influential salespeople therefore use this principle to their advantage, including many "psychological triggers" in their sales approach and presentations that influence customers throughout the sale. Of course, we never like to feel like we're being manipulated—that would create the opposite of the Heart & Mind connection we've been talking about. But these triggers, if used carefully, work so subtly we often don't know we're being influenced.

There are many triggers you can use to influence customers. In this chapter, I've identified the 7 triggers, or laws that, in my experience, have the most powerful effect on cementing customers' Hearts and Minds to yours during the sales transaction.

But please remember: Influence is power and, like The Force in *Star Wars*, some people abuse it. For the sake of your personal peace, your reputation and career, your loved ones, your company, and your customers, I urge you to use it **only** to *benefit* your customers and others.

Law #1. Invested Ownership: We value what we own.

When we invest time and energy in customers, we come to value them and care about them. Likewise, when customers invest time and energy working with us, they tend to develop affinity and trust for us. The more you can involve customers in the sales process, the more they value it. They become invested in the *outcome*, so they want to influence it. Then, when they find what they like, they grasp it. They feel ownership. Their Hearts and Minds are committed to buy. (That's ideal!)

You've likely noticed that children prize what they earn, but often neglect what's given to them. This explains why my son doesn't bring my car back cleaned and filled with gas. Yet, when he takes his car, he charges friends for gas and wipes off any dust! Because my son owns his own car, he naturally values and cares for it more than mine. That's how many people think. Humans have an instinctive need to care for what they own and an instinctive apathy for what they don't.

The Law of Invested Ownership involves time investment, as well as our monetary investment. In any situation, the more time and purpose we invest, the deeper we connect. Of the 7 Laws of Influence, this is the most powerful law to *positively* affect your customers. It's so powerful that when parties negotiate, the party who invests the most time senses the greatest loss if the negotiations fall apart and is more likely to back down or take a lesser deal.

To increase each customer's investment and sense of ownership, never *tell* a customer something you can *ask* her. The more opinions you ask for, the more investment she makes, and the more she begins to value you and your product. More importantly, she believes in her own answers more than anyone else's. Skilled salespeople are full of questions, inviting the customer to invest in the process by having to answer. A good teacher does the same thing when she asks her class, "In which year was the Magna Carta signed?" She knows the answer* (we hope), but it's the asking of the question which gives students ownership in the learning. Similarly, you can ask good questions, and lots of them, to increase your customer's ownership of the sales process.

It's like the old saying: "You can lead a horse to water, but you can't make him drink." So let him lead you instead!

Law #2. Give and Take: We feel obligated to return favors.

Have you ever received a small gift in the mail, like a bookmark or set of greeting cards or address labels with your name on them? If the gift is enclosed with a plea to send money and an envelope with a stamp, do you send money? If you don't, do you feel a bit guilty? If someone sends you a dollar bill for filling out a survey, can you, conscience-free, pocket the dollar without filling out the form? If I did something for you, you'll likely feel obligated to do something for me, wouldn't you?

Our common *need* to return a favor gives rise to the Law of Give and Take. We don't want anyone to think we are "moochers" who just take. The law

---

* In case you're wondering, the answer is 1215.

works. In selling, take advantage of it. Go out of your way to give customers a gift or do them a really big favor. Your customer will feel obligated to return the favor, or at least, just listen. It's kind of like the Second Law of Thermodynamics: You can't destroy energy; you can only move it somewhere else. And when you move positive energy to customers in any way, they will feel inclined to move it back to you—hopefully!—in the form of a purchase.

President Abraham Lincoln understood the Law of Give and Take: "If you would win a man to your cause, first convince him that you are his true friend. Therein is a drop of honey that catches his heart, which, say what he will, is the greatest highroad to his reason, and which, when once gained, you will find but little trouble in convincing his judgment of the justice of your cause, if indeed that cause be really a just one."[51]

I'm not telling you to start giving stuff away for nothing—that would be the equivalent of using too much Heart and not enough Mind. When you do something extra for a customer, you should *expect* her to want to do something for you in return. When she *offers*, you have proof that she recognizes your extra effort and believes you did it because you care about her. That's rapport.

Don't *dismiss* her desire to repay you for your sacrifice! At this moment, recall the favors you would want her to do for you: like you, trust you, buy your goods and services, refer friends to you, and be loyal to the company. When the customer thanks you for an extra service, you can respond in one of two ways:

If you say, "Oh, it was nothing. I do it for everyone," you're telling your customer that she's no one special. What a shock! She thought you *cared* about her. She was feeling affinity and trust in you. Did she read you wrong? Your dismissive answer sabotages the rapport you've built. It weakens your influence. It cheapens your gift. It lets the customer off the hook and cancels her obligation to you.

However, if you say, "Oh, you're welcome! You would do the same for me!" you reinforce both your special relationship and your customer's desire to repay you. You want customers to feel appreciative enough to buy, refer friends, and be loyal to you.

Never underestimate the power of giving great service. When you give love and loyalty, you receive love and loyalty back. This strategy is especially effective with Empathy-based buyers.

Law #3. Demonstrated Expertise: We trust authority.

Imagine that you're out shopping for a new oven and you go to two stores.

The first store is a big home appliance warehouse, with ovens, refrigerators, TVs, lawnmowers—everything you could possibly want for your house. Within minutes, you're approached by a 17-year-old sales rep named Sally. You tell Sally you're looking for a new, top-of-the-line stove. She takes you right over to the oven part of the store and you see there are many options to choose from. The choice is almost overwhelming. Sally seems nice and smart, so you ask Sally which one she recommends as the best model and she tells you, "Personally, I'd go with X brand. I hear it's really good."

You tell Sally you want to compare prices before you make your decision, so you drive to the next store. This store is called All About Kitchens. It only sells appliances for kitchens. When you walk in, you're immediately greeted by a 43-year-old woman named Judy. Judy is wearing an apron. She has just baked some cookies, which she offers you to try. You like Judy. She reminds you of your aunt. And she looks like someone who knows what to look for in an oven. You also tell Judy you're looking for ovens, and she asks "Gas or electronic?" You say gas. "Okay, well we have a model over here I personally recommend because I own one myself and I find that it cooks wonderfully." You notice the price tag on the oven and it costs nearly $200 more than you saw in the other store, but you take it anyway and, most importantly, you feel good about the purchase.

What you just experienced was the Law of Demonstrated Expertise in action. Who are you more likely to listen to for advice on which oven to purchase: the 17-year-old Sally or the 43-year-old Judy with "demonstrated" expertise in this area? Which store are you more likely to buy your oven from? The one that sells all kinds of appliances or the one that specializes in kitchens? You get the idea: Demonstrated Expertise sells.

Starbucks® has made an entire business out of this strategy. Everything about their stores is carefully orchestrated to communicate the fact that they are *experts* at coffee. From the Italian names "venti" and "grande" describing their cup sizes to the collection of different beans around the world they usually have on display near the counter, they've uniquely constructed a selling experience that triggers your *ClickWhirr* response for expertise and authority. They educate you about their coffee, and by educating you, they show you they are "the experts." That's more than Jim's Donuts down the block can say!

Your customer's trust in you increases automatically when she recognizes that you're an authority or expert. Your goal: Each customer says, "You're the expert; tell me what to do." The power of the Law of Demonstrated Expertise is the reason I included Expertise as a necessary ingredient of selling and serving successfully. As you would expect, authority especially influences Expertise-based customers.

However, it's not enough to *be* an expert. You must also *sound* and *look* like an expert. That's where the "Demonstrated" part comes in. Customers examine your appearance and your language. You'll undermine your authority in direct proportion to the amount of times you say "I don't know" or "Let me ask my manager" or "Let me check the book in the backroom." You'll also hurt your authority by dressing down and looking like a slob. Think of how much more of an authority and expert you look like when you wear a suit, rather than a button down shirt and jeans. The more expensive the product, the more of an expert you will have to be. So, unless you want your customers to see right through you, become an expert the easy way by first dressing and acting the part.

Law #4. Walking the Talk: We hate inconsistent behavior.

"But you promised!" Barely did the words escape his mouth then I felt that old familiar chill run up my spine. I was being called a liar.

What happened was this: My son wanted to borrow the car to take his friends to the beach. I had just had my car cleaned and I didn't really feel like letting my son and his friends spill sand and Doritos® all over my nice leather interior. I should have just said no; instead, I told him that if he cleaned out the garage and the cellar *and* raked the yard, then I'd let him have the car for sure. I thought that would be the deal killer. But sure enough, a few hours went by and my son came walking up to me with his palms out and a big grin on his face. I was astonished. "Let me get this straight. You cleaned the garage, and the basement, and you raked the yard? All by yourself?"

"You never said I had to do it by myself," he said. "I had my friends come over and help me do it. You always said, 'Many hands make light work...' now can I have the keys?"

"No," I said. "I still don't want you to take the car. I just had it cleaned. And...

"But you promised!" he interjected. Suddenly, I realized he was right. I had made him a promise, and as much as I wanted to go back on that promise, I just couldn't. How could I break a promise with him and expect to keep his trust? More importantly, what would he think of my character? Did I really want him to see me as someone who goes back on his word? So I lent him the keys and had *him* vacuum the sand and crumbs later.

What I experienced with my son was the Law of Walking the Talk. In a nutshell, this law holds that human beings desperately want to live up to the expectations others have of us and those we've set for ourselves. We want to be consistent. We want to "measure up." So, if someone expects us to keep our promise, we feel almost automatically pulled to keep it, even if it puts us in an inconvenient situation.

But it's not just about keeping your promises. For example, the other day a young man came up to me on the street and said, "You look like a smart and caring person, someone who values the environment and would do anything to protect it from the abuse of big business."

Right away, I thought, "Why, yes. I am a smart and caring person," but then I waited expectantly for what was coming next. The young man worked for an environmental non-profit and was soliciting donations to stop off-shore oil rigging. He was using a clever sales tactic that involved the Law of Walking the Talk. He was raising *my bar* to pressure me towards measuring up. Naturally, it worked. I gave him a buck and I really did feel *smarter* and *more caring* than the rest of my fellow men that day.

You can see how this Law of Influence works in your everyday sales approach. You make a hundred promises a day to customers, and they expect you to keep them. When you do what you say you'll do, customers learn you are trustworthy. Consistency produces even more sales than good selling skills. If you leave a gap between promise and performance, customers won't rely on you. So make no promise you can't keep. Then keep every promise. If you find you can't keep a commitment, call ahead to apologize. Follow that by doing whatever is necessary to make it right with the customer.

But also, seek ways to raise your customers' expectations of themselves. Do what the college kid on the street did to me: tell your customers that they are smart; remind them that they are kind and generous; and show them that they are conscientious, careful, and dedicated. Once you raise that bar, they will jump as high as you want, if only to be consistent with your high opinion of them.

Law #5. The Bandwagon Effect: We do what others do.

I have a friend who always hated red wine. Every once in a while, he would try a sip at a restaurant, but he thought it tasted awful. So, he stuck to beer. Then several years ago, the movie *Sideways*[52] came out. If you haven't seen it, it's about two friends who vacation in Napa's wine county for a week and try all sorts of wine and get into all kinds of crazy adventures. It's a funny movie. Well, a few weeks after the movie hit theaters, there were all sorts of stories on TV and the papers about how red wine sales were skyrocketing, especially for pinot noir, which is the star wine in the movie. People who hated wine or never really drank much of it were buying it by the bottle just because of the movie! I couldn't believe it. Sure enough, I went out with that same friend who hated red wine one night and noticed that even he was now drinking red wine. "Since when did you become a wine drinker?" I asked.

"It's going to sound silly," he said, "but I saw *Sideways* and saw how much the characters in the movie loved their wine, and I felt like I must have been giving it a bad rap all these years. It took me a while, but I finally found my taste for it!"

My friend (perhaps unknowingly) discovered the fifth Law of Influence: The Bandwagon Effect. You leverage this law when you promote your best-selling products: "This is our number one seller in this category!" This popularity lends credence to the product's claims. If so many people are buying it, it's probably good.

A similar tactic uses celebrity endorsements. Nike® sneakers took off when Michael Jordan started wearing and endorsing them.

As you would imagine, this law works particularly well on Enthusiasm-based buyers. They tend to be people-oriented, and make more impulsive (rather than logical) decisions.

A corollary of this law is the Law of Emotional Flow: Between two people, the one with the stronger emotion influences the one with the weaker emotion. In other words, the more passive person usually modifies his or her emotions to align with the more active person's emotions, not vice versa.

That's why your Enthusiasm affects everyone! If you inspire a customer with Enthusiasm for you and your products, she's more likely to inspire her friends.

Law #6. The Mirror Effect: We like people who are like us.

Even as tiny infants, we're fascinated by the sight of our own face in the mirror. This tendency towards vanity only gets stronger as we grow up.

As we said earlier, people are most comfortable with people like themselves. Marcus Tullius Cicero (106-43 BC) understood this 2000 years ago when he wrote, "A friend is, as it were, a second self." You wield more influence if the customer likes you. That's the whole point behind teaching the 4 E's and how to adapt your selling style to match with customers' buying styles. The more you can mirror your customers' own tendencies, the more they will feel a connection with you.

Don't you tend to like people who agree with your ideas, your politics, or even root for your own sports teams? I know I do. But I also know that in order to be a successful salesperson—in order to build that Heart & Mind connection—I must go out of my way to mirror my customers. This often means I have to change my sales approach and even my wardrobe. I've already made this point in earlier chapters, but it's such a powerful one that it bears repeating.

People not only buy from salespeople who are like them—they also buy from those salespeople they like. When a customer likes you, they feel more obligated to buy from you. Selling has been defined as the "art of being liked." The best way to get customers to like you is to like them and be like them.

Law #7. The Last One Left: We hate to miss out.

In the 1990s, I called this the Law of the Beanie Baby®. Other examples were the Cabbage Patch Kids® and Tickle Me Elmo® (you may substitute *any* product that limits the supply). This law is very simple: People attribute higher value to scarce or limited items.

The short supply increases demand because it implies that many people have decided it's a good product and want it. Not all scarcities are real, of course. Diamonds, for example, are not scarce because they're rare, but because the suppliers control their availability. Another example of this effect are those collector's issues of plates, dolls, coins, and model cars you see advertised all the time on TV, or most commonly, in the middle pages of *Reader's Digest*®. An ad like this might read: "Here's your chance to own a piece of history. Limited time offer—act fast. Three hundred Spanish coins dating from the 16th century were discovered in a sunken boat off the coast of Georgia. Only 20 coins remain. Act now and we'll include a free wall mount—but only to the first 10 customers." This may be an exaggerated example, but I think it's fairly typical of those kinds of ads that build a level of urgency and scarcity into their pitch. The advertisers are increasing your desire to purchase their products by increasing the urgency of the situation. They make you feel like there is this great offer to be had and if you act too slowly, you'll miss out forever. The truth often is there is no limited supply. Just wait a couple of weeks, and the limited time offer will be back again in another ad. But people don't want to take the chance.

Great salespeople know how to use to Law of the Last One Left to their advantage. They limit quantity to build value. In sales, the "take-away-now" technique works because of this law. It is especially effective with Ego-Drive buyers. But be careful: We've often been pressured by a pushy salesman to buy something because it's the last one left or because there are five other customers interested in buying it today. That kind of sales pitch reeks of the all-Mind salesperson we talked about in Part 1. If you're going to use this law in your sales presentation, do so sincerely. Make sure that the scarcity or limit is valid. Use this to manipulate and you will lose trust. Mention it as a matter-of-fact point the customer should be aware of. Camouflage the Mind approach with Heart by saying, *"The sale ends tomorrow. If this is the product you really want and is right for you, you can save money by making your decision before tomorrow. I don't want you to pay more than is necessary."*

Chapter 15

The Rules of Argumentation

"You can't win an argument, because if you lose,
you lose it; and if you win it, you lose it."

—Dale Carnegie,
How to Win Friends and Influence People[53]

The 7 Laws are just the beginning to harnessing the power of influence throughout your sales transactions. I believe you can become more influential by applying the Rules of Argumentation as well. Argumentation is not quarreling or bickering; rather, it's the methodical process of logical analysis. Argumentation is *effective* reasoning. Its appeal is to the customer's Mind, but in a way that is respectful of the Heart.

To deepen your influence, you need to think and speak in terms of the customer. You must acknowledge her predispositions and give reasons with those in mind. You must recognize that influence is non-coercive. It is reasonable and appealing, or it is nothing.

From the beginning to the end of the selling process, you make claims. Customers will heed your claims better when you make them under the Rules of Positive Argumentation (not coercive, manipulative, or deceitful argument). The Rules for Effective Resolution of Issues are:

- ♥ You and the customer share one goal: To find the products and services that best fit her desires, schedule, and budget—with no hidden agendas.
- ♥ Each of you is willing to accept what is true, regardless of your past understanding.
- ♥ You and the customer wish to resolve any disagreements—not merely settle them (as a compromise or surrender), but together find the resolution.
- ♥ Each of you has an equal opportunity to influence the other. One party's power or prestige does not influence the outcome.
- ♥ Both share the values of sincerity, efficiency, relevance, and clarity.
- ♥ Both are committed to nonviolence, freedom of speech, and intellectual pluralism (i.e., you can accept the validity of others' values, interpretations, and actions).

Oppositional Psychological Forces You Must Overcome

How often have you heard someone say, "You know, you're right and I'm completely wrong! I had never thought of it that way until you set me straight." Not very often, I'll bet! Usually the parties in a "debate" end up in a standoff, each the more convinced of his or her original position *by* the opposition.

Social scientists say that two psychological laws are at work to cause people to cling tenaciously to their opinions:

1. **Law of Investment Ownership: We value what we invest in.** It's one of the stronger "triggers" you can use to advance your sale. But it can also hurt you. Customers value what they invest in; therefore, customers feel *obliged* to defend positions they have valued. When customers object, they *own* the objection, and their investment has closed their minds. They consider it worth fighting for. Thus, your attempts to debate them are useless at best and offensive at worst. Debating alienates customers. They leave even more convinced that they are right and you are wrong.

2. **Law of Personal Defensiveness: I will defend myself against attacks on my statements because they're an attack on me.** Although it's not logical, my defense is emotional: If you disagree, you're calling me wrong and waging an assault against me. So, customers mount their defenses and close their minds against your influence. Feeling personally attacked, they fight or flee, depending on their buying style.

These two laws inform us that we won't influence customers' opinions until *they've* opened—or reopened—their minds to us. Since people lock their minds from the inside, you won't succeed by applying force or pressure from the outside. *They* have to unlock their minds. It's their decision.

How can you influence them to open their own minds? Heart is the magic key. As you'll remember, Heart means seeing another's viewpoint and feeling the issue as *she* feels it. Although you may disagree with her viewpoint, she won't reopen herself to you until you *feel* genuine Heart **and** she *recognizes* your Heart. Once she believes you understand her, she can unlock her mind to your influence.

Notice this paradox: If you want to influence someone, you have to first listen and be influenced *by* that person. Influence doesn't come with silver-tongued speech. It grows from listening carefully and then seeking to understand. Listening with Heart opens Hearts *and* Minds, while offensive tactics force customers to defend themselves. Heart melts, offense breaks.

Bill Brooks of The Brooks Group, a North Carolina sales consulting company, found that if the customer opens her mind after it's been closed, you have a 91 percent chance of making the sale.[54] Bill attains this high closing rate because he also sells according to his customers' buying styles.

When customers resolve their own doubts, they can dismiss their concerns. They can wholly erase their original *negative objections*, and replace them with what they see as their own *positive objectives* for buying.

Here's another bonus: Won-over objectors are more likely to become your advocates. They will probably tell friends how much they have learned from you and how much they enjoy your wonderful products and services.

Remember that customer objections dissolve only from the inside.

Affirmative Defenses

An affirmative defense is an objection to your claim that *you* bring up. You raise it before the customer does in hopes of defusing it. You can use Heart to strengthen your affirmative defenses. Used well, affirmative defenses can yield several benefits:

- ♥ When *you* bring up a product's potential downside, you build trust. Customers realize you won't say anything just to make a sale.
- ♥ It's better to frame your defense, and then answer it. The buyer's version may be more difficult to answer.
- ♥ You gain a tactical home-field advantage when you raise the issue.

If you wait until your customer raises it, *she* owns it. If she owns it, she feels obligated to defend it.

The best method for handling sales resistance is to *prevent* it in the first place. Affirmative defense is a reliable tactic for doing so.

It's a winning battlefield technique too. Chinese Chairman Mao Tse-Tung told his military leaders, "The only successful generals in the world are those who can accurately anticipate the strategic actions of their opponents and therefore tactically outmaneuver them."

When should you use an affirmative defense? Generally, it's effective for objections that buyers commonly make and is less effective for those they rarely make.

How can you anticipate their objections? The number of objections is finite. Great salespeople identify and anticipate the common ones—product limitations, price, terms, delivery, etc.—and work them into their sales presentations. For other objections, they develop a standard response.

Quick Tips to Open Your Customer's Heart and Mind

- ♥ Make your successes visible. Let your physical appearance and face demonstrate your abilities and enjoyment of selling. Offer ideas to your company to upgrade the showroom to better reflect its stability and success.
- ♥ During the conversation, use the customer's name and the word *you* more often than *I* or *we*.
- ♥ Mirror the customer's behavior and words. Match your pace to hers to help her feel at ease with you.
- ♥ Clarify the customer's options, and present all of them as smart. Of course, you can imagine that, for her, some are smarter than

others. (To do this, you'll have to know the products better than the customer does.)

♥ Build anticipation. Great salespeople personalize their presentations: "Just think how great you'll feel, how good your home will look, what compliments you'll hear..." You can't stir up much of a Heart & Mind connection if you don't make the purchase personal.

♥ Show that real people manage this store by using the active voice. Say, "We've reduced the price of this brand by 50 percent" rather than "The price of this brand *has been* reduced by 50 percent."

♥ In response to an objection, first mention the areas of mutual agreement. Point out all areas of agreement before you present an opposing idea.

♥ Be *for*, not against, products and concepts. When expressing a different point of view or explaining why your product is better than the competition's, give positive reasons for your view rather than arguments against the other.

♥ Be definite in your hopes. Use *when* rather than *if*: "*When* you see our product work..." Use *will* rather than *would* or, better yet, use *do*: "I *will* look for you again tomorrow" or "I *do* look forward to seeing you again tomorrow," not "I *would* like to see you again tomorrow." Use *can* rather than *could*: "Yes, I *can* do that" rather than "I *could* do that."

♥ If price becomes an important issue, offer an incentive. Remember, an occasional gift never hurts when you're using Heart & Mind.

Chapter 16

The Two Master Skills of Heart & Mind

*"I am the world's worst salesman; therefore,
I must make it easy for people to buy."*

—F. W. Woolworth (1852-1919),
founder of Woolworth's®

Recently, an insurance company's sales manager puzzled over the sharp drop in policy sales by new agents at the 18-month mark. Was it burnout? Or had they exhausted their list of friends to solicit? The company investigated and found neither was the case; rather, sales dropped because their agents felt less need to listen. When they were new, they were teachable and open-minded. They listened to their customers' stories until they understood the whole situation. Only then did they recommend insurance products best suited to their clients. On average, the customer took more than an hour to describe their situation. However, after the agents had worked for 15 to 18 months, most of them had discovered that customers' situations fit into a limited number of categories. They could ask only a few key questions and, within 15 minutes, they knew in which needs category their customer fit. Once they had their client pegged, they stopped asking and listening and began recommending.

These salespeople thought the purpose of their opening questions was only to help them discover customers' needs so they could recommend the right product. It wasn't. Good questions are as important to the customer as they are to the salesperson! While the salespeople may have correctly analyzed their customers' needs, their closing percentages dropped. The customers needed to feel understood. They wanted the salespeople to connect with their hearts, not just offer a product!

The Power of Being Understood

My research has found that there is no other tool more critical to a salesperson than asking questions and then listening to the answer. In fact, the key principle of Heart & Mind Selling is to never say a thing that you can find a way to ask. Why? Because:

- ♥ **Good questions position you as a trusted consultant**. When you ask questions, customers feel you trust them. They believe you want *them* to provide the answers and the content. Feeling your trustworthiness, they open up to your influence. All Heart & Mind relationships start with trust.

- ♥ **Good questions help customers discover their own needs and make their own decisions.** Remember the first Law of Influence—the Law of Invested Ownership? We value what we own. Targeted questions give customers ownership of the buying process. They help customers explain their needs and feelings, clarify their thoughts, and hit the target they want without *your* leading them. For example, "To help me understand completely, why is that quality/feature important to you?" or "What did you like best about your last product of this type? What did you like least?" Since you inquired with Empathy, the customer retains buy-in control and draws her own conclusions. Since it's her idea, it must be good and, as a result, she wants to buy from you—naturally!

♥ **Good questions clarify customers' thoughts.** Your questions help customers decide the four major issues (after they've decided to work with you and buy from your company). These questions apply to all major purchases:

1. Aesthetic/fashion decision: What color? What style? What look? How will it match? Will it make my house more beautiful?

2. Performance decision: How will it perform? How long will it last? How easy will it be to clean and take care of?

3. Priority decision: How soon do I want to have it? When do I really need it?

4. Budget decision: How much will it cost? Is it worth the price?

Which of these four decisions is most important? That depends on the customer, so your first goal is to find out her decision-making priorities. How do you get her to tell you?

You guessed it—ask questions!

Useful Questions to Ask

It has been said that sellers who ask prospects a series of questions average many more sales than those who ask fewer questions. If you were able to dramatically increase your sales, how would that affect you and your family?

Imagine what might happen if you asked each shopper seven or more open-ended or tie-down questions. Open-ended questions require more than a yes or no answer. They require an explanation, so they *open* the customer to say what she feels. Tie-down questions limit the answer to yes or no. For example, "You said stain resistance is important to you, correct?" (tie-down question). When she says yes, the next question is open-ended: "Why?"

Consider asking the following questions to help your customers open up and clarify their thoughts. I've phrased these questions for floor coverings (because it's the industry I come from), but you can easily adapt them to your product and services.

Questions about priority:
- ♥ Why are you looking to purchase new floor coverings?
- ♥ What did you like best about your last carpet? What did you like least?
- ♥ Which rooms are you thinking of covering?
- ♥ What is your time frame for purchasing your carpet?

Questions about performance:
- ♥ Do you have children? How many? How old are they?
- ♥ Do you have pets? How many? What kind?
- ♥ What kind of traffic does each room experience: light, medium, or heavy?
- ♥ How long would you like your new floor covering to last or look new?
- ♥ What are your long-term expectations?
- ♥ What kinds of warranties are important to you?

Questions about aesthetics:
- 💜 What look or style of floor covering do you like?
- 💜 Are you looking for a formal style or something more casual?
- 💜 What do you want color to do for you? Make the area feel spacious or cozy? Make the room feel warmer or cooler?
- 💜 What colors will look best in that room?
- 💜 Multicolored and textured carpets can help hide soiling or stains. Do you feel that will be important?

Questions about budget:
- 💜 Many of our customers are using our credit program. Would you like to sign up for our card? (If your store has a credit program, you should advise each customer of it near the beginning of your conversation.)
- 💜 What size are your rooms? How many square feet do you want to cover?
- 💜 What budget do you have in mind? (Note: This is the next-to-last question on this list. I recommend that you ask in this order.)
- 💜 If I understand correctly, you have about ___ square feet to cover and a budget of around $___. That gives you a good range of products to choose from. You could pick products up to about $___ per square foot.

By using these questions regularly and truly listening to the answers, you will raise your sales percentages.

Of course, you will want paper and pen to record her desires. A customer might say that the floor covering in another room is getting older, but doesn't need replacing yet. Knowing that, you can follow up with the customer to cover those rooms later. Writing down her desires gives you two added benefits:

1. You can send a thank-you note: "Thanks for coming in. I enjoyed working with you on your carpet needs."
2. You increase her affinity for and trust in you. Seeing you record her desires, she realizes how much you care about what she wants.

The goal of business, we agreed, is to make and keep customers. With this information, you can retain these customers as your "personal trade." They become a source of profitable business for you in the short-term *and* in the long-term.

Improve Your Listening

In school, kids are taught the three R's. I wish they would add an L, because few of us know how to really listen. More than 2000 years ago, Epictetus, a Roman slave, philosopher, and author of *The Art of Living,* noted that nature gave us one tongue and two ears so we might hear from others twice as much as we speak.[55]

Listening really goes hand in hand with questioning as a master skill of Heart & Mind Selling. Without being an effective listener, you can't possibly retain or evaluate the information you're getting from your questions. You're also not going to be able to pick up on the subtle hints customers give you that indicate their preferred buying style.

Let's say you're dealing with a customer who is looking to buy a new stereo. You notice that she speaks very slowly, taking a long time to consider what she is about to say. You notice that her voice is soft and tending towards a monotone. You also notice that she talks a lot about her family—it's clear that she is someone who defines herself by the relationships and important people in her life.

What kind of buyer is she? You might gather from listening that she is an Empathy buyer. If you listen closely to all your customers, not just to their words, but their pace and tone, you will pick up hints that will allow you to adjust and adapt on the fly.

As you improve your listening skills, you also extend your influence. A Russian proverb states, "If you want to influence someone, use your ears." Dean Rusk clarified: "One of the best ways to persuade others is with your ears—by listening to them."[56] As salespeople, we can often gain greater results from listening than we can by speaking out. Sometimes we communicate better when we let customers and ideas speak for themselves. Consider these two examples:

1. The November 11, 1996 issue of *Fortune* magazine reported a study of top achieving salespeople at 70 large companies. The study, conducted by the New York-based consulting firm The Ron Volper Group, found that the ability to listen is the biggest difference between "solid" and "average" sellers. Top performers allow customers to do about 70 percent of the talking in a typical sales call.[57]

2. (This example removes salespeople from the sale altogether, so don't let your boss see it.) In 1998, as Dell® Computers was preparing its website to sell computers and accessories without human help, the executives worried that buyers would purchase less expensive computers if they had no guidance and influence from salespeople. They were surprised to see, however, that most people actually bought higher-priced systems on the web than they did when shopping over the phone. The website's silence allowed people to talk themselves into something without someone talking them out of it!

When you stop to think about it, it's amazing how hard it is to shut up. We've been taught all our lives to feel uncomfortable with silence and to move the conversation along at all costs. While this is certainly important in the sales transaction, it's also critically important to know when to bite your tongue. As the old saying goes, "Silence can be golden."

As a salesperson, realize you actually have more power by not saying a word. The more you speak, the more you commit yourself to positions that may not align with your customers' wants or buying style. It's better to have them make the first moves, and then work from whatever they say to help them come to the realization that they need your product and or service.

Biting your tongue is certainly hard for some people—especially Enthusiasts! My advice is to count to ten after a customer finishes speaking before starting to speak. This will help you avoid stepping on their words, but most importantly, make sure they've had a chance to say everything on their mind. Like a good detective or CIA operative, your task is to gather as much information as you can in a very limited amount of time. The more time and space you allow for your customer to talk, the more likely they are going to fill that space with something of value to you. As my mother always said, "If you're too busy talking, you're too busy not listening." Learn to shut up and get out of your own way!

The Four Facets of Effective Listening

Effective listening is *more* than receiving sound waves. It's active, energetic, discerning, and involved. Good listening includes:

- ♥ **Sensing.** Listen carefully to what the customer says *and* what she doesn't say. Practice recognizing and appreciating silent messages like facial expressions, body language, vocal intonation, choice of words, processing style, personality style, etc.
- ♥ **Attending.** Send verbal, tonal, and visual messages to the speaker to indicate your attentiveness. Use eye contact and nod your head.

Use body language that shows you are open and receptive. Use short, affirming words that don't interrupt, such as "yes…go on… I see."

- ♥ **Responding.** Ask for her feedback. Do you accurately understand her words and feelings? Paraphrase, clarify, and verify.
- ♥ **Weighing.** Decide fairly. How much should you be influenced by what you heard?

As a seminar presenter, I know for sure that *listeners* greatly influence *speakers*, not just vice versa. When I present to a group of cooperative, responsive listeners, I exceed even my own expectations. I have more of an effect on them. They receive a more stimulating, meaningful message. I affirm what Thoreau wrote, "It takes two to share a truth: one to speak and another to hear."

The Four Levels of Listeners
Which are you?

1. **Non-listener**: Makes no effort to hear what's being said, and is mostly concerned with getting a chance to speak. The non-listener is so busy preparing what to say *next* that he or she can't listen to what's being said *now*.

2. **Marginal listener**: Hears sounds and words, but doesn't comprehend the speaker's message. The speaker *thinks* this person is involved and attending, but the attention is just an appearance, not reality. The marginal listener tends to stay on the surface of the conversation. Often, that leads to misunderstandings.

3. **Evaluative listener**: Actively seeks to comprehend what the speaker is saying, but doesn't make an effort to understand the speaker's unspoken intent or feelings. Tends to be a logical listener, more concerned about content than feelings. Evaluative listeners can parrot the speaker's words back, but haven't evalu-

ated the message. This listener may form an opinion before the speaker's message is completed.

4. **Active listener**: Seriously and consciously attempts to see things from the speaker's point of view. Listens not only for content, but also for the speaker's intent and feelings. Listens for how things are being said. Perceives what is *not* being said. With this listener, all the components of Heart & Mind are at work: being open-minded, responsive, attentive, sensitive, and nonjudgmental. It requires a lot of practice to become an active listener.

Elements of Effective Listening

The following elements of effective listening were compiled by author and speaker Dr. Ralph G. Nichols, known as the Father of The Field of Listening. He finds that effective listeners:

- Invest themselves in the topic; they are engaged in the exchange, whether or not they speak.
- Adjust to those addressing them.
- Hear the speaker out; they wait until they understand a point before passing judgment.
- Set details aside until they catch the main idea.
- Use the time lag between the usual speaking rate (125 words per minute) and the usual comprehension speed (three times that or more) to recap the message in their mind, and to adjust their responses to the current context.[58]

It takes full concentration to understand the connotations or implications of a speaker's words. Don't assume you'll catch them without effort. *Search* for the speaker's meaning and implication. The 500 most commonly used English words have 14,070 dictionary meanings. (The word "set" has 464 meanings!)[59] A skilled speaker uses nuance and inflection to communicate, and you may miss part of the meaning if you drift away.

How Well Do You Listen?

Answer the questions below. "Yes" means you definitely need to work on your listening skills (What you think of as a skill may actually *handicap* your listening ability!); "No" indicates good listening skills; "DK" (Don't Know) means you need to ask a friend or co-worker so you *will* know.

Do you often:	Yes	No	DK
1. Use the excess time between people's talking speed and your listening speed to think about other things while you're trying to keep track of the conversation?			
2. Listen primarily for facts or details, rather than main ideas?			
3. Avoid listening to ideas you think might be difficult to understand?			
4. Decide from a person's appearance and delivery that the speaker won't have anything worthwhile to say?			
5. Try to make people think you're paying attention when you're not?			
6. Allow certain words, phrases, or mannerisms to prejudice you so you can't listen objectively?			
7. Turn your thoughts to other subjects when you believe a speaker will have nothing particularly interesting to say?			
8. Interrupt people when you're puzzled or annoyed by what they say?			
9. Stop listening because the message is dull, or because you don't know or like the speaker, or because you've heard it all before?			
10. Interrupt before people can express their complete thoughts?			

Do you often:	Yes	No	DK
11. Listen for hidden meanings?			
12. Daydream while people are talking?			
13. Forget to write down the important details of an agreement?			
14. Get distracted by other sights and sounds?			
15. Try to speed up conversations?			
16. Have to ask people to repeat information because you missed it?			
17. Get angry or excited when a speaker's views differ from yours?			
18. Believe you can complete routine tasks while listening and not miss what's being said?			

A Final Word

Listening gets people to listen to you. That's another paradox. The salespeople of the past were good talkers. They could sell ice cubes to Eskimos, hair to barbers, and dirt to farmers. However, smooth talking and fancy words don't close sales—listening and asking questions do. Remind yourself that everything the customer says is fascinating. Remember, the secret to being interesting is being interested!

Part IV.

Putting
Heart & Mind in
Your Selling Approach

*In this section, you will learn how to apply the
four-step Heart & Mind sales process*

Chapter 17

Step One: Creating Rapport

*"It is not the customer's job to remember you.
It is your obligation and responsibility to make sure
they don't have the chance to forget you."*

—Patricia Fripp, Business speaker[60]

In Part I, you were introduced to the Heart & Mind philosophy. In Part II, you learned the internal changes you need to make before you can become a Heart & Mind salesperson. And in Part III, you read about tools you can incorporate into your sales approach to better understand your customers and make a Heart & Mind connection. Now it's time to put it all together in the four-step Heart & Mind sales process:

- ❤ **Step 1: Creating Rapport**
- ❤ **Step 2: Engaging the Customer**
- ❤ **Step 3: Presenting a Tailored Package**
- ❤ **Step 4: Signing the Loyalty Contract**

Let's begin with Step 1…

♥   ♥   ♥

Building a Heart & Mind customer doesn't happen overnight. You have to start somewhere small. For most salespeople, this means approaching customers on the sales floor, in person, or even over the phone and simply grabbing their attention—getting them to take five minutes out of their busy lives to stop and listen.

The challenge? Most customers will enter your store or business hoping to buy from you, but not expecting to like you. They consider salespeople their *adversaries*. My friend is a perfect example. He thinks every salesperson is lying to him in order to get his money, so he's naturally abrasive and defensive when he's approached in a store or on the phone by a salesperson.

When dealing with customers such as my friend, the odds are heavily stacked against you from the very beginning. You desperately want just a second of their time to show them you're honest and trustworthy, but they won't give you the time of day. Think about your own reaction every time you get a call from a telemarketer trying to get you to subscribe to some magazine or donate some money to a charity. How long do you give them before you hang up? You're facing a similar obstacle with your customers every day. Thanks to increasing bombardment of marketing and sales messages customers receive every day, it's getting harder and harder for you to break through the noise and earn their attention and trust. It's getting increasingly more difficult to make that initial connection, let alone create a long-term relationship!

In this chapter, I'm going to describe how you can soften your customers' Hearts and Minds until they accept you as their advisor and not just another salesperson. Once you've achieved this goal, you've successfully created rapport—that's the moment when they've committed to you the time and attention you need to educate them more about the products and services you're offering. Fail at this step, and your sale is dead in the water with little hope of being revived. Succeed and you've done 95 percent of the heavy lifting it takes to close the sale and make a loyal customer for life!

Making the Connection

According to The Brooks Group, a consumer research organization, a shopper will grant you a 90-second "trial."[61] That's how fast typical consumers decide whether they'll like working with you and want to buy from you.

Your opening statements and initial impression usually determine whether this shopper decides to listen to you or walk out. We've already established that today's consumers are wary of salespeople. Most put up defenses as they enter your store, so your approach must entice them to lower their guard.

Shoppers *maintain* their defenses when they feel the salesperson:
- ♥ Is too aggressive or "slippery."
- ♥ Is not available to answer questions.
- ♥ Can't answer questions about the products.
- ♥ Tries to sell them the wrong product.
- ♥ Ignores them, or is indifferent to them.
- ♥ Doesn't build rapport immediately.

In summary, shoppers:
- ♥ *Shake off* salespeople who are untrustworthy, ignorant, indifferent, or unfriendly.
- ♥ *Adopt* salespeople who are trustworthy, knowledgeable, empathetic, and friendly.

How do your closest friends rate you on those last four qualities?

Fortunately, you can take active steps to avoid your customers' concerns:

- ♥ **Approach customers from the side**, so they won't feel intimidated, overpowered, or confronted. Customers perceive the space directly in front of them as their own. Don't violate it. Come alongside to help them.

- ♥ **Be spontaneous.** Avoid the trite "May I help you?" Your first words should have nothing to do with the business at hand. Say something that uniquely fits this shopper and this moment. Your spontaneity will make you genuine.

  You can develop spontaneity by practicing. Start conversations with strangers in elevators, supermarkets, and restaurants; it will become easier and more natural for you. I make it a goal to have at least one conversation with a stranger every day. I find that the more I do it, the more confident I feel.

  Think of openings that will differentiate you. You want to catch your customers' attention in a *positive* way. You may reuse your "different" idea, just don't use the same words every time. No matter how good you are, a *set* speech will sound insincere and uncaring.

- ♥ **Notice and comment about something unique.** Use the love language of *affirming words*. You might mention your customers' clothing, shoes, handbag, car, or jewelry. You could comment on how well they've managed in the difficult weather. Or mention their children: "Your daughter is so (cute/bright/alert/gracious). How old is she?" Parents read you as sincere when you compliment the child's behavior. They'll glow when you say (if it's true), "She's really well behaved!"

If you find commonalities between you, talk briefly about them. Make your remarks appropriate, of course—warm, without invading privacy. Avoid false, insincere, or excessive praise. Obvious flattery *destroys* rapport because it's manipulative.

- ❤ **Introduce yourself on a personal basis.** Remember that your customers are looking for an experience, not just a trade of their money for your product. Extend your arm as soon as they say hello and shake hands firmly, but not for too long. Help them remember your name by wearing a nametag on your right shoulder (it's easier to read that way), and by introducing yourself clearly and warmly. Learn and use their names when you greet them, again during your presentation, and again when you part: "Kay [or Mrs. Jones], thanks for spending this time with me. I really feel good about your decision."

Calling customers by their names works magic. As lecturer and author Dale Carnegie said, "If you want to win friends, make it a point to remember them. If you remember my name, you pay me a subtle compliment; you indicate that I have made an impression on you. Remember my name and you add to my feeling of importance."[62]

- ❤ **Besides a handshake, find other ways to touch appropriately.** Touch is one of the five love languages, remember? Of course, you want to touch only in ways comfortable to the shopper. Be careful and sensitive. Watch your customers' body language to see if they withdraw in any way. Look for their need for personal space. By observing, you can decide whether a light touch on the arm would be appropriate or unwelcome. (Consult the 4 E's to know which customers want to be touched and which ones prefer their distance!)

- ♥ **Connect and bridge to business**. Use questions like, "What's the special occasion?" or "What brings you in today?" or "What are you looking for today?" Maybe simply go ahead and beat them to the punch: "I bet you just want to look." Be ready with a soft comeback if they agree: "Looking is fun. May I ask what you are looking for?"

Your goal is to connect. If your customers insist on looking by themselves instead of connecting, offer a helpful suggestion and then leave their space. Stay close by (straighten up a display or put back samples), but give them the room they want. Don't continue to chatter, just be there when they have questions. They will let you know when they are ready to talk.

- ♥ **When they're ready to talk, start by asking questions.** Perhaps a series of multiple-choice questions: *Vinyl or wood? Traditional monitor or LCD? Standard definition or HD? Solid color or pattern?* Such multiple-choice questions don't threaten. These questions encourage customers to talk because they are factual and allow customers to protect themselves if need be.

If customers look confused when they see the wide variety of products or new features, you might show your Empathy by saying, "Confusing, huh? It was confusing for me at first too! But actually, you have just three basic choices to make. I can explain those to you."

Or you might ask for their opinions on a special item. "We just received this new line of canary-yellow washers and dryers. I'm interested in your opinion of them."

Once customers start talking, they will become more comfortable with you and the process. The more your customers voice their needs, values, and concerns, the better *understood* they will feel. And when they feel understood, they'll gradually open themselves up to your influence.

♥ **Then listen.** As we've said, listening to others makes them feel understood and cared for. It opens them further to your influence—but only if you are giving them your full attention. If you ask your customers a question they've already answered, any rapport you've carefully built up will quickly disappear. Likewise, if you answer an unasked question, they will stop asking. Respond precisely and fully to their comments and questions. Tell them only what they need or want to know.

♥ **Respond with Empathy.** If you've experienced what your customers are feeling, tell them that you understand. (If *you* haven't experienced it, you can describe the experience of another customer or friend.) Tell them how you and others handled the issue.

If they don't open up and begin sharing personal information, it's a good sign that they don't like you or don't trust you. You will know that your tactics are not working. Do something else to check their buying style.

♥ **Remember that customers are fallible, but they hold the power of purchase.** The old adage "The customer is always right" isn't *always* true. Occasionally, customers mistake facts, misjudge value, or behave rudely. Some customers don't realize that they don't know what they want. Your task is to correct their mistakes, yet not offend them, so you maintain rapport.

Before you disagree with a customer, be certain of your facts. The customer will consider you an expert only if you are credible. One slip and credibility vanishes. But you always need to be tactful. If the customer judges you to be arrogant, you may lose the sale. You can't impose your will. Customers have the ultimate power: They choose whether to buy from you or walk away.

This challenge—teaching customers without upsetting them—can keep the best of us on alert and aware of our need to improve! Customers are the lifeblood of your business, so you must treat them as VIPs.

You Control the *Process*; Let Customers Control the *Content*

Practice the techniques above, and hopefully you will have convinced customers that you're an advocate, not an adversary. This means that they:

- ♥ Know you're more concerned about what they need than what you would like to sell.
- ♥ Feel safe with you. You can tell them (gently) when you think they're heading toward a decision that isn't in their best interests. You should feel confident enough to disagree, and they should feel confident enough to really listen.
- ♥ Can rely on your word. They know that you'll tell them, in advance, if you can't meet their requests or time frame.
- ♥ Consider you an expert, and can rely on your answers.
- ♥ Are open to your ideas. You've built the rapport and trust that will allow them to lead them through the sales transaction and onto the

next step: the engaged exchange.

Before we go on, however, a final word: The Heart & Mind system I'm recommending is not smoke and mirrors. It's not *pretended* friendship and trust you're offering your customers. It's real friendship and true trustworthiness. When these are authentic, they sell. If they aren't, they fail. I don't recommend pretense.

You should plan to *lead* customers through the sales transaction. You're the expert, so you know how to do it most efficiently and suitably for each customer. Customers expect your Expertise and leadership.

However, you want to lead only the *process*. You want customers to control the *content*. You want them to know *they're* in charge of options and decisions. You're a useful guide, but no more. You can control the sales process by suggesting the sequence of steps and asking questions. When you ask questions and agree with your customers' answers, they'll know they're making the decisions and controlling the content.

Throughout the sales process, encourage your customers to give feedback and voice any problems. That alone will differentiate you! Of all dissatisfied customers, typically only 4 percent tell the company. The other 96 percent never tell the company; they just tell their friends. Amazingly, your *inviting* complaints makes customers more loyal. How is that possible? Complainers complain because they have faith that your company cares and will fix the problem. Most are company patriots, and want to help the company do better. (Of course, if you don't treat their complaint with proper respect, you'll lose their loyalty.)

Here's the kind of complaints you can expect:
- ❤ I didn't get what I expected.
- ❤ A salesperson was rude to me on the phone or in person.

♥   I felt neglected, and no one seemed to listen to my concerns.

♥   The salesperson projected a *can't-do* or *who-cares* attitude.

According to customer service studies, customer loyalty increases:

♥   When you invite complaints. So seek them out. And welcome them when they come.

♥   When you promise to investigate the problem and promptly solve it. Treat every complaint as significant.

♥   When you do solve the problem immediately.

That's why I encourage you to consider every complaint as an opportunity to show customers what you can do.

How many times will you be tested today? And how many times will you succeed in earning or renewing the respect and allegiance of another customer? Every time you deal with a customer, it's *all* on the line: Your organization's reputation; its investment in facilities, products, and services; its staff; and even its future. So win the Hearts and Minds of every customer today. Make them customers for life!

Chapter 18

Step Two: Engaging the Customer

"If a man empties his purse into his head, no man can take it away from him. An investment in knowledge always pays the best interest."

—Benjamin Franklin

Once you sense rapport with your customer, you can move to the next step, which is to suggest that the two of you "engage" in a product hunt. You offer her your product Expertise, your Empathy for her needs, your Ego-Drive to fulfill her desires, and your Enthusiasm for doing it all with her. You suggest that the two of you pool your knowledge and experiences, collaborate on the search, and seek to find products and services that suit her.

The basic procedure for an engaged exchange with a customer is a Q & A. You ask questions, she tells you what she prefers. We call this an "engaged exchange of information." If you're in rapport, your customer will likely accept your proposed engagement.

If you sense you're not yet in rapport, you have two choices: backtrack and build toward rapport again, or go ahead and propose the engagement. If you go ahead and she accepts, she is giving you another opportunity to show that you are likable and trustworthy. She's not sure yet. You may yet achieve rapport with her. If she declines your offer, you're out. (You could introduce her to another salesperson who might click better with her feelings.)

Remember, however, my primary claim in this book: If the customer still feels no rapport with you by the time you want her to sign the contract, she's unlikely to sign. It takes Heart and Mind to reach agreement. Connecting with reason alone makes fewer sales. So, sometime before you ask her to sign, she needs to feel affinity and trust.

Exchange Information to Uncover Desires

As Mark Twain said, "It's a terrible death to be talked to death." The late newsman Eric Sevareid would have added, "It's like being nibbled to death by ducks!" Yet the best way you can uncover your customer's buying priorities is to invite her to talk.

What we don't know *can* hurt us. If we fail to find out what's on our customer's mind, she either won't buy from us, or she won't be a happy buyer.

To maintain your control of this segment of the process, be prepared with questions that will elicit the customer's true feelings and dreams. At this stage, your primary aim is to elicit information. Your challenge is to hear her words and glean information from her clues, as a detective does.

In an engaged exchange, you should ask questions whenever you can, and avoid telling. Telling is not selling!

Sometimes this inquiry process is called discovering, qualifying, or probing. I don't like the word "probing," because it sounds like something extraterrestrials do to earthlings on their spacecraft! You and I would resist, and resent, this process. So will your customers unless you handle questions especially well.

I prefer the term "engaged exchange" to describe the ideal process. The dictionary defines exchange as "a mutual expression of views" and "giving something in return for something received." An exchange is a sharing of information—a conversation of questions and answers from both directions.

In selling, we use engaged to mean involved. When you're engaged, you wholly engross yourself in the exchange. You focus your full attention, mind, and energy on the customer.

It's not hard to engage myself with a customer. I find it fascinating and fun to learn about other people. Of course, your engagement must be so genuine that the customer feels that whatever she says is fascinating, and that you want her to tell you more. When you do this well, the customer thinks you're the most interesting person she's ever met.

In turn, your challenge is to fully engage your customer. Good questions build rapport while keeping your customer involved. The right questions guide your customer to make her own right decision. (In the process, you'll be forced to do less nibbling and more listening!)

Benefits of an Engaged Exchange

In sales, as well in our personal relationships, asking questions establishes trust, gives us information, and helps people focus on their needs. An engaged exchange keeps customers listening, involved, and invested. It makes them feel that all judgments and decisions are theirs. Best of all, the information you gather allows you to personalize your presentation to suit your customer's unique needs, wants, and values.

But keep in mind that this is not a game of 20 Questions. Avoid too many rapid-fire inquiries and any questions that may upset or irritate your customers.

It's harder to ask questions than it is to give information. But I know for a fact it produces far more customer rapport and higher closing rates. Let's discuss some of these benefits in greater detail:

You naturally care more because you're investing energy in learning your customer's desires. When you set aside your agenda and work to understand hers, you must invest thought and feelings. As you engage yourself in your customer's needs, you naturally care more—and your caring isn't forced. Its voluntary nature will show, and your customer will feel validated. The Law of Give and Take may even kick in, causing the customer to become more engaged and care about you too.

An engaged exchange extracts the customer's wants and needs from her brain. A doctor who would diagnose an ailment and write a prescription without first asking thorough questions and conducting an extensive exam would be guilty of malpractice. Well, so would you! You can't remodel a product to match a customer, but you can emphasize different features and benefits.

An engaged exchange keeps your customer focused. You're in for a tough time if she tunes you out. The quickest way to lose your customer is to stop asking questions. When people become confused, their thoughts wander. As long as customers are answering your questions, they are listening, which requires focus, which in turn leads to understanding the benefits—and eventually, to a sale.

An engaged exchange empowers the customer. Customers feel they are in control when you ask questions with Empathy. You are clarifying, and they are confirming. They feel confident when they are providing the information and directing the content. An engaged exchange is the opposite of manipulation.

As you exchange engaged questions and answers, you can often determine whether your customer is analytical and fact-based (right-brain) or creative and imaginative (left-brain). These terms relate to how we process information. (They also relate to our analysis of personality, selling, and buying styles.)

The brain's left hemisphere handles analytical thought and language, while the right hemisphere is in charge of creativity and intuition. While everyone can use both sides, most individuals are more comfortable using one hemisphere than the other.

A right-brain customer has an easier time visualizing how a room will look after it has been decorated. A left-brain customer tends to rely more on details and specifications. A left-brainer is likely to say "I think," while a right-brainer is more likely to say "I feel." Knowing which side of the brain each customer favors helps you determine which products might fill her needs and how to present those products. Let's take a closer look at what it means to be a left-brain or a right-brain customer:

Left-Brain Customer	Right-Brain Customer
Good at languages	Good at conversation
Objective (black, white)	Subjective (gray, colors)
Quantitative	Qualitative
Logical	Emotional
Stays in the lines	Creative
Goal-oriented	Principle-oriented
Analyzes	Intuits
Remembers words, pictures, faces	Remembers tunes, names
Thinks in sequence	Thinks creatively
Predicts prosperity (glass half full)	Predicts scarcity (glass half empty)
Focuses internally	Focuses externally
Short-term thinking	Long-term thinking
Likes to be managed	Likes to lead
Focuses on one thing at a time	Often does many things at once
Prefers straight-forward approach	Comfortable with ambiguity
Deals in information	Deals in hunches
Prefers the practical value	Prefers aesthetic values
Uses minimal facial expression	Uses many facial expressions

63

Remember, every customer buys for two reasons: the logical reason and the real (often emotional) reason. They might be the same, but one may be based in the left brain and one in the right.

An engaged exchange leads customers to their own conclusions. Effective questions help customers recognize their needs and wants and understand the possible solutions. Feeling confident with that new understanding, they can draw their own conclusions. When they do, they'll buy at higher price points than when they suspect they've been manipulated by the salesperson.

An engaged exchange leads customers to buy-in. You know your exchange has been successful when your customer begins talking about the products and services. She begins to relish ownership. Because she wants it, she forms a commitment to the product. The customer's commitment is strong, because it was her idea. She owns it, so it's good! As the customer talks, three things happen:

1. The customer naturally identifies which features she likes.
2. The customer measures the product's value for her purposes.
3. The customer anticipates benefits she will receive.

The opposite of an engaged exchange is an "expert's selection." If you know your products well, you may sense—perhaps even sooner than the customer does—which products best match her desires. Drawing on your Expertise, you could select a product for her. This method usually fails, however.

Even if your intentions are pure (to match the customer's best interests), most customers will suspect you are "pushing" a product or manipulating their decision to promote your interests. When customers suspect manipulation, they withdraw their rapport and pull away. They ignore you and work to regain control. Some openly rebel; others politely walk out. Nagging doesn't work! Spend an hour with a small child and you'll know what I mean. Your success will come when you ask engaging questions, let customers feel in control, and help them find their "want to."

Once You're Engaged, Seek to Understand the Customer

Plan your questions for the engaged exchange to correspond to the questions the customer is naturally asking herself:

♥ Have you been honorable with me? Have you respected, trusted, and believed me?

- ♥ Where are you going? What's your vision of this search for my product?
- ♥ Are you coming with me on the search? Are you willing to accompany me at my level, to learn with me and support me as I work to find a solution?
- ♥ Will you be patient with me? Will you accept my mistakes with compassion?

The customer hopes that the two of you will consider the products' relative benefits together and decide on the best one collectively. The customer wants you to advise her. That's optimal for you—because it's your goal as well!

Be Alert and Focused

Here are some practical ways you can actively engage yourself with the customer:

- ♥ Make eye contact. Looking directly at the customer shows your interest and concern. Stand near her. Don't look around while she's speaking, stare at the floor, look over her head at someone or something else, or consult your watch.
- ♥ Nod and use appropriate facial expressions. Don't just stand and stare at her! Let her know you're involved.
- ♥ Look friendly and smile when you hear something you like.
- ♥ Clarify and paraphrase when you're not sure what the customer means or wants. Do the same when you're not sure she knows what you mean.
- ♥ Ask open questions: who, what, where, when, why, how. These questions allow customers to restate, and even rethink, their positions.
- ♥ Tell her what you don't know about her desires. Ask her to fill you in.

♥ Avoid distracting actions or gestures. Become aware of your mannerisms and idiosyncrasies that may distract her from your message.

♥ Don't interrupt!

Offer Nonjudgmental Responses

We are naturally critical of others when the things they value, their personalities, and their buying styles contrast with our own. It's difficult to avoid negatively judging such responses. These guidelines may help you avoid showing any negative reactions toward your customer, and help you use the differences to the customer's (and ultimately your) advantage:

♥ Respond to the customer's behavior or idea, not the customer. Don't let the issue become a personal or personality matter.

♥ Respond in the present, not in the past. You can't do anything about the past. You can only deal with the present and work to control the future. Put your focus where it belongs.

♥ Respond by *describing*, not *evaluating*. Describe what's being said, not your opinion about what's being said or the person who said it. Show objectivity.

♥ Use "I" messages to tell your customer how you feel. The "I" message rephrases the customer's statement in your own words. Thus, you won't come off as judgmental, only as sharing your opinion. If she tells a long story about her neighbor's list of problems with the solar roof in her kitchen, your recapping "I" message could be: "*I* understand that you think solar roofs can be problematic. *I'm* aware of those problems. *I've* seen some brands work very well in the right location, however."

♥ Use a "feeling" question. A feeling question can work when an "I" message isn't enough. Reflect your customer's feelings and reasons as you understand them: "You're *feeling* [an emotion] because [of a reason]. So you *feel* you wouldn't like a solar roof because of the problems your neighbor has had with hers?" Keep your own feelings in check and use this strategy to clarify the customer's meaning.

Useful phrases when you think your perceptions are accurate:	Useful phrases when you're not sure:
It appears that you feel…	Could it be that…?
So from your point of view…	I wonder if…?
So it seems to you…	Would you buy this idea?
It seems as though, in your experience…	I'm not sure if I'm with you, but…
So from where you stand…	I would like to try paraphrasing your words.
It sounds like you see the issue as…	Does it sound reasonable that you…?
So you think…?	Is it possible that…?
So where you're coming from is…	Correct me if I'm wrong, but…
What I hear you saying is…	Could this be what's going on?
It sounds like you're [emotion]…	From where I stand, you seem…

Practice These Skills

The skills of focusing, listening, and understanding are just that—skills. You can't expect to perform them better until you practice them. We all understand that we can't play the piano skillfully unless we have lots of practice. The same is true of selling skills.

Pick one or two techniques and practice with customers, co-workers, friends, and family members. You may never master the piano version of Mozart's "Linz" Symphony, but you can fine-tune your focusing, listening, and understanding skills.

You will want to continue your engaged exchange until you understand your customers' desires, and they recognize that you understand them. When you reach that mutual understanding, you can begin to collect products you believe will best fulfill their desires.

The Power of Knowledge and Choice

Have you ever tried to convince a 6-year-old to go to bed? If you had only three reasons why he should and he countered with four objections, you were in trouble! He had even more control if you couldn't respond to any of his objections. He would simply apply the Law of Requisite Variety, which governs every negotiation: The person who has the most alternatives (or toy/car/machine with the most options) has the most control.

Recall the oft-used statement: "Knowledge is power." Knowledge creates power because it offers choices. Expanding your choices also expands your strength, especially in negotiations. The more you learn about your opponent's motives, needs, wants, strategies, and tactics, the more you can control the negotiation. (But remember, the customer is not the enemy!)

This law applies to all aspects of life. Many people are unhappy, worried, stressed, or miserable because they feel they lack choices and control over their situations. This sense of "no control" makes people feel helpless or victimized. And when people feel helpless, they usually do nothing!

By contrast, when we believe we have many choices, we feel more in charge and more empowered. Perhaps we could improve the quote by changing it from "knowledge is power" to "choice is power." Most psychologists agree that being "out of control" is the primary reason for stress, negativity, low self-confidence, and feelings of inferiority. These negatives cause many people to seek counseling or buy self-help books. They are searching for alternative methods for dealing with their life.

How does the Law of Requisite Variety govern your selling efforts? First, knowledge can expand choices for both buyer and seller. For instance, if you know only one way to handle price objections and your customer knows more than one way to object, you can expect the customer to win. With a limited variety of responses, you will close fewer deals. The mindset of salespeople toward their products—their biases against some and for others—is so common that I address it during every sales seminar. I ask, "How many of you have favorite products?" With their best be-kind-to-dumb-animals look, they answer, "We all have favorite products!"

When I ask why, I get answers like:

- ♥ I can genuinely endorse only products I like and believe in.
- ♥ I would feel dishonest selling something I didn't believe in.
- ♥ I like to share my experience. I can tell shoppers that other customers like how the product looks and feels in their homes.
- ♥ I'm more credible because I can speak from experience when I promise that certain floorings will look good for a long time.
- ♥ I want my customers to have the best, so I promote products that have given me no problems.

Their answers are right…yet wrong! First, salespeople are right to want to be genuine—to promote only what they believe in. I know the feeling. Early in my career, I tried to sell life insurance. Since I had canceled my own life insurance policies (because when I die, I want it to be a R-E-A-L tragedy), I couldn't do it. How could I sell insurance if I didn't have any myself? Long-term success in selling requires that salespeople believe in their products.

However, belief alone isn't enough. It's only half of Enthusiasm, one of the four characteristics of high performance. The other half is conveying your conviction that the product's value exceeds its cost through powerful words, corresponding body language, and obvious passion.

Your passion and Enthusiasm come through when you believe in:

- ♥ Yourself.
- ♥ Your company.
- ♥ Your product.
- ♥ The value of the customer.

Your customers feel your conviction, either consciously or subconsciously, and that positively shapes their emotions. (Remember that all buying decisions are first emotional and then justified with logic. Some people even buy what makes no logical sense, because their emotions are so strong.) The customer's positive emotions, even though subconscious, move her to buy!

Yes, believing in products—having favorite products, if you will—and conveying your belief are two parts of Enthusiasm. But just as belief alone doesn't sell, neither does Enthusiasm. It must be balanced with Expertise. Salespeople must know the value of every product on the showroom floor so they have more choices to sell.

In my seminars, my next question is: "How many favorite products do you have?" Typically, the answer is four or five. But one study found that salespeople who favored only four to five products sold half as much as those who favored six to eight products. And those who had six to eight favorites sold half as much as those who had nine to twelve. Having only a few favorites sabotages sales!

A sales pro can honestly sell anything on the floor to the right customer. Every product you carry has a place—it has good points, features, and benefits. I recommend that you examine all the products in your show-room that you don't like (or think you don't like). Ask others about them, because the owner carries them for a reason. Once you've learned the value and best uses for each product, you can enthusiastically and honestly sell them for their proper application. When you are convinced about the value of each product, you can sell it.

Then, as you approach a new customer, set aside your product-enthusiasm and express only your customer-enthusiasm—the privilege of meeting a new friend and helping her. At this point, you should be product-neutral. Your primary job is to discover this customer's needs and find the right product for her. It's about finding a product for a need, rather than a need for a product.

Granted, 80 percent of our sales come from 20 percent of our products. But salespeople get in trouble when they assume that their next customer will want one of the top 20 percent. I've observed thousands of sales-people. Those who favor few products ask their customers few questions. (The fewer the preferred products, the fewer the questions.) Too soon, they assume they know this customer's needs and start presenting a product. What does assuming do? It makes an a** of you and me, and it depresses sales. There is an a** for every seat!

Their mistake reminds me of the sales training video we used several years ago in our carpet sales training. In it, a woman customer carries a hidden camera in her purse while shopping in several stores. The video shows how unsuspecting salespeople react to her needs. As each salesperson ap-proaches her, she shows a sample of an inexpensive carpet. (The sample looked like Texas—a lot of wide-open spaces.) She tells the salespeople, "My friend put this carpet in her home. I really like it. I've just painted my living room and I'm thinking of buying the same carpet." Then she asks, "Is this a good carpet?" and waits.

Most salespeople responded to her question with an answer instead of a question. They described the sample's poor grade, explained that it wouldn't serve her needs, and offered her a higher quality. Not one salesperson asked, "Before I can tell you whether this is a good product or not, please tell me where you are going to put it. What's the traffic in that room? Tell me your long-term expectations."

The video's lesson is that all the salespeople wrongly assumed that the customer wanted a high quality carpet. They didn't leave their minds open to the possibility that she wanted or needed something more economical. When a salesperson assumes the customer's needs and tells her what she wants, the customer thinks, "The salesperson's trying to sell me something." As we said earlier, customers trust salespeople who ask questions—and then listen.

When you know more about your customers' buying motives, you can better structure benefit statements and sell more products! Answer these questions for yourself to determine where you might need to improve your knowledge:

- ♥ How many more sales could you close if you could appeal to a personality type opposite to yours? Or to the needs of all 4 E's?
- ♥ Do you understand how women buy and how their approach differs from men's?
- ♥ Do you know how the wants and needs of today's shoppers differ from yesterday's shoppers? In many cases, techniques that worked well then no longer work now. Have you updated your toolbox? How?
- ♥ If you could learn more about competing products, could you position yours in a more favorable light?

Think of yourself as a perpetual learner. Learn to read, and then read to learn. Learning will expand your choices. Knowledge is power!

Result: The Customer Recognizes That You Want to Fulfill Her Best Interests

When you've properly managed the relationship with your customer, she will feel affinity for you, trust you, and believe that you want to fulfill her best interests, not yours. With those powerful incentives, she'll likely value the product options you present. That's the best setting for the next step in the sales process: your product presentation.

Chapter 19

Step Three: Presenting a Tailored Package

"Ask and it shall be given you; seek and ye shall find; knock and it shall be opened unto you."

—Matthew 7:7

Through your engaged exchange, you have, hopefully, made your customer feel understood and free to open herself to your influence. You've sold yourself by seeking to understand her needs and wants. You have applied both Enthusiasm and Expertise to convey your conviction. You've discovered what the customer values. You know what she wants and why.

Now it's show time! You will present products with features and benefits that you have tailored to what the customer values. You will thoughtfully promote those benefits that are consistent with her needs and wants. Your presentation will help the customer select a product and feel good about it, because she realizes that the information you've gathered suits her uniquely. Your extensive product knowledge will answer her questions in ways she understands.

Now, to shift from the question mode of the engaged exchange to the product presentation, try saying something like:

- ♥ Based on what you've told me, I have several products I think are just what you're looking for. May I show them to you?
- ♥ I think I now understand what's important to you. I have several products I think you're going to love. Would you like to see them?

Whenever possible, show the customer more than one product, but never more than four. More options tend to confuse the customer. Only one option may cause her to think that you're pushing a product, and she has no choice. Today's customers need to feel like they made a decision without being told what to buy.

Be Careful With Your Claims

Throughout the sales process, you've been building your credibility. Don't squander it on false product claims. If the customer feels you are over-promising, it destroys trust. In presentations, you make four types of claims. All of them must be right for the customer.

1. **Facts**. These are your descriptions of products, features, services, warranties, installation, competitors, and the like.
2. **Definitions**. These are your interpretations of terms and concepts—what they include and exclude, and how you place them into categories.
3. **Value**. These are your judgments as to worth or value. For customers, you evaluate characteristics, such as the usefulness, longevity, fashion, and ease of maintenance of products; available services;

manufacturer comparisons; and the relative merits of competing products or services.

4. **Policy**. These are actions. You decide what to advise the customer to do.

As you discuss each product, credibility demands that you can argue both for and against it. You must know its advantages and limitations.

You increase your credibility when you can argue not just factually, but also emotionally, from both sides. You'll be more credible when you are able to advocate Product A from its standpoint—its advantages and the disadvantages you will concede. Turning around, you must be able to advocate Product B from its standpoint. What are its advantages, and which disadvantages will you concede? When you can factually and emotionally argue both sides of an issue, you discover the strength of each position. That makes you sound product-neutral and more credible. (Of course, you may hold strong opinions about the comparative value and which product the customer should select. But at that point, you want to sound neutral, so the customer feels she's making the decision based on the truth of both positions.)

Compare the Features and Benefits of Fitting Products

Some 95 percent of what's sold isn't what the buyers want. It's a means to getting what they want. People don't buy things, they buy results: happiness, popularity, comfort, attractiveness, saving money, saving time, easier ways to do things. They buy gold for what it can buy them, not for its shine. Don't sell me a steak! Sell me sizzle, quality, taste, etc.

Here's an example to help you distinguish the two concepts: Last year, Home Depot® and Lowe's® sold millions of quarter-inch drill bits, but I propose that none of the buyers wanted a quarter-inch drill bit. What they wanted was a quarter-inch hole! The bit was a means to an end. A strong, sharp bit was the feature; a clean hole was the benefit.

Think about this possible exchange between a customer and car salesperson. Which of the two statements would have more impact for a customer?

1. This car has memory built into its antilock brakes.
2. This car's antilock breaks will help you stop on a dime when you need to so you can avoid an accident.

A consumer typically responds to the first statement with a blank stare. She thinks, "So what? Why should I care?" The second statement has meaning for customers. They can understand what's in it for them when they choose this car. When we realize that a product can directly benefit us, we usually want it.

Benefits describe the customer using the product in a pleasant and successful situation. Thus, your promotion of benefits brings your products to life! The customer can imagine gaining the advantage.

So, early on, you should address your customer's important self-interest question: "What's in it for me?" Help the customer understand that buying this product promotes her best interest. During the engaged exchange, you discovered the features she deems important. Now show her the payoff benefits that match her desires.

Product features differ from benefits. Features describe the design or qualities of a product—what it is.

Customers don't buy features; they buy benefits (although salespeople often confuse the two). Always lead with a benefit and follow with features—show the customer what the product will do for her, then what it is. Start your product presentation by explaining how a benefit will meet one of the customer's values: "I think you'll like this product because..." or "One of the nice things about this product is..." In order to finish the sentence, you have to know the difference between a feature and a benefit.

Most customers can't translate product features into user benefits on their own. So features mean nothing to customers unless they can see how the benefits help them achieve their purpose. Average salespeople sell features instead of benefits. Often, they emphasize features because: (1) the manufacturer trained them—the features differentiating their product from its competitor are important to manufacturers and (2) they want to tell customers what they know.

Average salespeople tend to tell customers too much—they "throw up" everything they know in an effort to establish Expertise. If we tell customers all we know, we usually confuse them. Adding to the confusion, average salespeople also use industry jargon: "This carpet is a 1/10 gauge and has 6.5 turns per tuft." A real expert knows when to turn it on, and when to turn it off.

So, how much should you tell your customers? Only what they want to know! Customers are looking for enough information to make a comfortable decision. If a customer is an Expertise buyer, she may value some technical information. If so, she'll give you plenty of signals. These buyers want details and education. Others may want little or no technical information.

Give each customer what she wants! Don't show her the engine if all she cares about is the leather interior. Don't demonstrate child-restraining seats if she has no children! Remember, consumers don't buy features—they buy the benefits that features provide.

Build Customer Anticipation

After you've discovered what results your customer wants, light up her imagination with visions of how your product fulfills the end she has in mind.

As a kid, you probably discovered that anticipation could be better than the real thing! Think of your birthday or Christmas or Hanukah. As the day approached, your excitement grew. Sometimes, however, after opening your presents, the reality was less wonderful. Remember your anticipation and employ that power. Don't worry about letdown. If the customer buys what she really wants, she won't feel it.

You can ignite a customer's desire to own a product by employing Enthusiasm to enliven questions that build her anticipation. For example:

- ♥ Can you imagine how relaxed you'll be after a day floating on a raft in your backyard pool? The week's stress will float away.
- ♥ Can you imagine the feeling of being away from the world on a deserted island that you sailed to in this new boat?

As you explain how your product can fulfill his dreams, you help the customers build his own desire for ownership. (Of course, your questions must relate to truth. Don't lose your credibility here.)

Activate the Customer's Senses

All salespeople rely on customers' sense of hearing to convince prospects that their product or service is the best. What separates Heart & Mind salespeople from the rest of the pack is their ability to appeal to customers' other four senses: sight, touch, taste, and smell. When you can let your customers visualize how they will enjoy your product, when you paint word pictures with colors and details, you turn these pictures into mental "color photos" that become sales tools for you.

All five senses can help customers convince themselves that your offer is superior. Once they come to that conclusion, buying becomes much easier for them. Do you go beyond telling them about your products or services? Do you make every effort to let them experience it themselves? Are you activating all your customers' senses to the fullest? Are you always looking for better ways to involve customers in your presentation?

Place a check in front of things you do, and leave the other statements blank.

_____ I use colorful pictures and photographs to arouse customer interest.

_____ I use charts, graphics, and performance data to illustrate my products.

_____ Where appropriate, I get my product physically into my customer's hands.

_____ Whenever possible, I use demonstrations to increase my customer's understanding of my product or service.

_____ I encourage my customers to take apart, use, and otherwise thoroughly inspect my product.

_____ I make an effort to use all five of my senses to get a complete picture of my customer's surroundings.

Salespeople who appeal to all five senses benefit far more than those who rely on hearing alone. Seek to learn which of the senses each customer relates to best (see earlier chapters on the 4 E's). Then emphasize this sense in your presentation.

Propose a Union of Customer, Company, and Product

If you've followed the steps of the Heart & Mind system, you've built rapport with the customer. You've shown Empathy, Ego-Drive, Enthusiasm, and Expertise. You have spent time in an engaged exchange with your customer that led you to care about and trust each other. You've focused on benefits important to the customer. You have demonstrated your product the way the customer wanted it demonstrated.

Since you've built credibility, sensory pleasure, and optimistic anticipation, and you have offered her the choice of several products that meet her desires, she likes you and trusts you. (At this point, trust is more critical than affinity, because you want the customer to have faith in your recommendation, not just you.) She's open to hear your recommendation of the best option for her.

Here's an example: "I really think this product will fill your needs and enrich your home as you wanted. In my opinion, it's the best choice for you. More importantly, however, which of these options do you think will best brighten your home?"

To reinforce your case, when you state your recommendation, you'll want to summarize the benefits she wanted and the unique benefits that you and your company offer her.

The customer is now ready for you to invite her to make her third decision: Which product shall I buy?

Chapter 20

Step Four: Closing the Sale

"Friendship implies loyalty, esteem, cordiality, sympathy, affection, [as well as] readiness to aid, to help, to stick with, to fight for, if need be."

—B. C. Forbes (1880-1954),
founder of *Forbes* magazine[69]

Once you know how to A-C-T (see Chapter 7), and know what your customer wants, you need to muster the courage to ask for the order. When we were children, you and I naturally asked for what we wanted. Somewhere between childhood and adulthood, something made us stop being open to asking without guilt. Out of a fear to ask, adults often sabotage their own happiness and potential.

There have been many times when I've been afraid to ask. I haven't asked for upgrades in hotels and airlines, for time off work, for second servings, for higher fees, and more. And I've lost out. Legendary hockey player Wayne Gretzky said, "You miss 100% of the shots you never take,"[64] and I've now learned that the more often I ask, the more often I win.

Our natural reluctance to ask for something in our personal lives spills over into our sales efforts. Fear of rejection is painful; actual rejection hurts like the dickens. Sometimes pride holds us back instead of fear, or low self-esteem convinces us we're not worthy.

Whatever your excuse, you can't shift the responsibility for the close to your customer! Salespeople who pass the buck this way don't seem to close many sales. Once in a while, a customer may give you the order without asking, but most will not. Knowing that customers, deep inside, want to decide and take the product home, peak-performing salespeople will ask. So ask!

You can also personalize your closing question. If you have rapport and your customer has shown hesitancy, but you know she emotionally craves a product, you might say with a smile, "Why don't you boldly do it?"

In sales training classes, instructors spend a good deal of time teaching closing techniques. In practice, however, your closing should be a minor part of the transaction. The close happens naturally when you have:

- ♥ Created rapport.
- ♥ Built a trust relationship.
- ♥ Sought to understand the customer through an engaged exchange.
- ♥ Presented a package that meets the customer's desires.
- ♥ Given a convincing feature-benefit demonstration.

When you're in rapport with a customer, you can sense whether she wants to close. When she does, ask her. Yes, even customers in rapport may not offer to purchase without being asked. Customers need the subtle pressure that comes with a verbal or nonverbal request from the salesperson.

Psychologically, customers respond better when the salesperson expects them to say yes. Consequently, the pros sell more because they believe every customer will buy from them. They are genuinely surprised when a customer doesn't. We tend to get what we expect.

By assuming the sale, you can ask politely, sincerely, confidently, and with eye contact. When you believe your customer will buy, you won't be fazed by any objections. When a customer says no to the first attempt to close, successful salespeople view it as an opening to move closer to the sale. They interpret their customer's objections not as a no, but rather as a plea for more information. Believing that's her motive, these salespeople immediately look deeper into the objection. After they address it, they ask for the close again. Great salespeople ask repeatedly.

It's been said that peak performers ask for the close an average of five times, while average salespeople ask only once before giving up. In the end, the only people who fail are those who don't try again—and again when necessary.

Look your customer in the eye and ask, "Ready to sign the agreement?" Then hush! Wait. Expect questions.

Know When to Keep Quiet

In every negotiation, there's a time to talk...and a time to listen. If you can learn to use silence to your benefit, and not just because you're afraid to speak up, you'll have an edge. After asking for the order, Heart & Mind salespeople wait for a response, no matter how long the silence lasts. They understand that silence gives the customer time to think. It also adds subtle pressure because most people find silence uncomfortable. It invites them to decide.

In addition, if the customer has an unspoken concern, the silence allows her space to divulge her real reason for hesitating.

Counsel Your Customer as She Considers Her Options

Some customers will say, "Yes, let's do it." You respond, "That's a good decision," and repeat the reasons that they have made the right choice for them. You're ready to sign the agreement and make vows of mutual loyalty. (These topics will be explored further in Chapter 20.)

Other customers will pause, because they can't quite decide. They need a consultant again. Likely their indecision is rational, not emotional. They may want to rehearse the reasons. They want to talk, and bounce their reactions off your empathetic listening ear.

If you've properly built rapport with your customer, you will know that she remains your ally and emotionally wants the product. She considers you her consultant, because you understand her needs, have good will, are knowledgeable, and are anxious to help her improve her home. Still, be prepared to serve as a collaborator in the decision. Not an advocate, but a guide who has nothing but good will toward the customer.

Look for three types of pre-commitment questions:

1. **Understanding.** The first type of question is to help customers be sure they understand the rational reasons for buying this product. This is the easiest for you, and confirms that you've built rapport. The customer wants to be able to respond knowledgeably and persuasively to her spouse and friends, who may not share her emotional commitment to the product. These questions will be "softballs" from a friendly source. You can answer them with confidence and use your affinity to reassure her.

2. **Pre-Commitment Jitters.** The second type of question comes

up when the customer gets cold feet. She's thinking, "I love this couch, but will I love it five years from now?...Will the color really go with that chair?...Will I have to repaint the walls?" She wants reassurance. The best you can offer is your value judgment and the rational reasons for buying. If you're in rapport, she will feel calmer and reassured. If you're not in rapport, she'll need more coaching from you, and may want her spouse's or friend's approval as well.

3. **Objection.** The third type of question is an objection. She may dislike some feature of the product, or may want one product that combines the benefits of two (when that combination is not available). Or she may object to the price.

The Real Selling Begins With No

Handling objections is an advanced skill, attained only by master salespeople. It requires confidence, expertise, insight, patience, and hope. Objections separate the order-takers of the world from the salespeople! You will need your best selling skills at this critical moment.

"Overcoming objections" is a popular topic for sales books and seminars. Some recommend the tactic of battering an objection into submission. I don't recommend it. You may win the battle, but lose the war. The customer may concede, but walk out.

Average salespeople seldom overcome customer objections, because they don't understand the psychology of influence. They mistakenly believe that great salespeople have a way with words and can "sell ice cubes to Eskimos." Believing that, they may resort to a frontal attack, spout contrary facts, articulate polished arguments, or argue forcefully. I prefer to leverage the natural laws of human behavior, as we discussed earlier.

When your customer asks you a hardball question, she's more likely to believe your response when you show confidence, not surprise or doubt. That shouldn't be difficult. You shouldn't be surprised, because you should know nearly every objection a customer may raise and be ready to answer it. You shouldn't doubt, because you should already know the tradeoffs of buying these products. What the customer desires may not be available, or not be available in her price range.

How you defend objections corresponds to your natural selling style. If your primary selling style is Ego-Drive, it's hard to remove yourself from the sales equation. Faced with opposition and the choices of fight or flight, Ego-Drive salespeople will usually choose to fight when someone says no.

Empathy-based salespeople tend to cave in when opposed, and they often choose flight when they hear no.

Enthusiasm-based salespeople tend to push emotions when faced with opposition. That may connect if your customer's objection is emotional. If not, your emotions won't speak to the objection.

Expertise-based salespeople will reply with strong reasons. That response will work if the customer's objection accurately reflects how she feels. However, stated objections often camouflage another objection, or a fear that she is too embarrassed to express. Your Expertise will miss the target.

Once you adopt the attitude that objections are not setbacks but opportunities—once you learn that selling actually begins when the customer says no—you can act confidently. You can leverage the Laws of Influence. They tell us that your challenge is not to convince the customer, but to help her to convince herself. People may doubt another person's facts and opinions, but they seldom question their own.

To achieve the customer's inside-out conviction, you need to first learn what her real objection is. Regardless of your selling style, you must resist your natural response to tell the customer she's wrong. Don't "object back." Take care not to put her on the defensive. Rather, listen carefully.

Use your Empathy to neutralize her defensive instinct to either argue or withdraw. In sales, we call the process "cushioning." When we listen intently and can honestly tell the customer, "I understand how you feel because…," we gain the most influence, and the customer is most likely to drop her defense. The key is to clarify and verify.

Clarify

Years ago, super salesman Bill Gove introduced the concept of harmonizing objections in order to clarify. He suggested we begin our response with the customer's facts and perspective. Examine them. Ask questions rather than shut them down. Guide customers to solve their own concerns. He taught salespeople how to harmonize objections by using "Feel-Felt-Found" to express Empathy: "I know how you *feel*. In fact, I originally *felt* that way too. Can I show you what I *found*?"

Let's suppose your customer says, "I believe I need to think about the purchase." A pro recognizes that statement as a clue that something else is bothering her. Your strategy is to find out why she needs to think about it. Seek to understand both what she said and what she may be feeling and hiding.

A salesperson whose selling style naturally lacks Empathy might ask, "Why do you need to think about it?" That's often too aggressive. Instead, try, "I understand how you feel, because you're going to live with this a long time. This is a big decision. I would want to be sure too."

Or you can use a "their-a-phrase"—say what you heard her say, except in your own words. Repeat her concerns accurately and without bias or a hint of disbelief: "What you're saying is that you need to talk it over with your husband, because you're not totally sure about it right now." Their-a-phrasing makes a customer feel more comfortable.

Once she senses your continuing Empathy, she'll usually listen to your next question. (She'll interpret it as your sincere wish to clarify.) You might ask, "What's your biggest concern?" or "I've found that customers who need to think about it often have something bothering them. Is there something I haven't explained enough?" If she doesn't respond, you could continue with, "Knowing you a little, I'm sure you have a reason for feeling the way you do. May I ask what it is?"

Your harmonizing with the customer cushions her defensiveness. If there were an Operator's Manual for this technique, it would warn: To be successful, you can't follow the cushion with "but" or "however." Can you imagine hearing, "I love you, but…" or "You look nice. However…"? To say, "I understand how you feel, but…" tells people you haven't understood at all. Whatever follows the "but" and "however" usually negates everything before that.

Cushioning is usually the surest way to move a customer to reveal the real concern. Once you've clarified the real reason, you two can discuss her objection objectively instead of objectionably!

Verify

Once you sense clarity, you're ready for the next step. You still need to know whether she's revealed the real reason—all of it.

Memorize these two sentences: "Obviously you have a reason for feeling this way. May I ask what it is?" Asking permission leaves the customer in control.

Is this direct question too assertive? Seldom. You wouldn't be offended if someone asked you "why" in this way, would you?

Now here's a powerful way to verify the real issue: "If you weren't concerned about [their stated reason], is this the product you would buy?" For example, the customer said the price is too high. You can ask, "If you weren't concerned about the price, is this the product you would buy?" If the customer says, "Yes, I love the product," you have verified that price is the real issue. You might offer financing or layaway, suggest your 90-days-same-as-cash program, show her it's only a few cents more a day for what she really wants, or other solutions.

If she says, "I have to talk it over with my husband," you might verify by asking, "If you weren't concerned about talking it over with your husband, is this the product you would buy?" You'll know soon whether the husband is the real objection.

This question helps her reveal whether she thinks the product is right for her. If you allowed the customer to leave the store without clarifying and verifying, you would never know what the true issue was. She may well go to another store where someone else will become her friend—all because you failed to ask these two questions:

1. Surely you have a reason for feeling this way. May I ask what it is?
2. If you weren't concerned about…(or, if…weren't an issue to you), is this the product you would buy?

Verify, because you can't answer the objection if you don't know what it really is. Remember: The way we see the problem is the problem!

Ways to Respond to Real Objections

The following methods for handling objections work better in some situations than others. I recommend that you practice them until you can use them with no trouble.

- ♥ **Denial.** The only time to deny an objection is when the customer's statement is clearly wrong. For example, a customer questions your store's integrity and you know it's untrue. If she says, "I've heard you don't take care of complaints," you may respond, "Well, Mrs. Smith, I don't think that's true. Whenever a customer complains, we work with her. We always strive to take care of our customers. We want them all to feel well served, so they can recommend us to others. That's how we've stayed in business so long. We'll do the same for you." Or show that her objection does not apply in this case. Or that her objection is relatively trivial.

- ♥ **Reversal.** "Turn the tables." Turning their objection into a reason to buy can be powerful. By doing so, you show the customer how her position actually benefits her. Here are a couple examples: A customer called and said, "Sam, I can't attend the seminar tomorrow. We're too busy." I reversed her objection: "If you're too busy to break away for a while, that's the very reason you need this class. You could probably gain more time for your customers if you used the time-management techniques we teach." Another customer says, "Business is so slow that we can't afford the seminar." You might respond, "That's the very reason you need to come!" Just remember that you're not entitled to use reversal until your customer feels your Empathy.

- ♥ **Reframing.** Put the customer's objection in a different light with the Feel–Felt–Found system. To review, when the customer says the price is too high, you may reply, "I understand how you *feel*.

I *felt* the same way when I first saw it. Then I *found* out about all the benefits. Did you know it comes with this, this, this, and this? I realized it was a bargain once I *found* out all it could do!" Reframe the objections and build value.

- ❤ **Confirmation of the benefits.** When a customer says the price is too high, what is she really telling you? Why didn't she just turn on her heel and walk out? It's because she likes you and your company. She prefers to do business with you. By not leaving and continuing to talk with you, she's saying, "I think I can get it cheaper elsewhere, but I would rather get it from you. Tell me why yours is worth more." The customer wants to hear a good reason because she wants to buy from you—like her emotions are telling her to do.

- ❤ **Pointing out the dilemma.** Say something like, "Yes, you're right. You can't buy wood flooring that is dent-proof. It's the nature of wood. When you want wood, you take it with that risk. When you look at the other floor coverings we have and compare them with wood, which do you think would look and work better in your home?" You clarify that she must choose between two alternatives, neither of which is ideal. Then let the customer choose.

- ❤ **Dissociate.** Show the separation between reality and appearance. Regard them as unconnected.

Dealing With Price Issues

If you're selling products on price, you're headed for bankruptcy. You must shift the customer away from price comparisons. People just want, naturally, to pay the lowest price you'll accept. So price is seldom the main issue in your customers' purchasing decisions; it's merely a decision-influencer, not a decision-maker.

Price really matters to only a few buyers. Nearly all customers care more about relevance, fashion, and function. But they want these for a good value—a fair trade of money for the products and services. Therefore, when you hear a price objection, use the techniques described above. Ferret out whether price is the real reason. If so, focus on the value you add that no one else can offer this customer.

Here are some other ways to deal with price issues:

- **Acknowledge the difference.** Look the customer in the eye and say, "You're right. Our price is higher, and it's worth it because [state a benefit that matches this customer's desires]." You need to know all the reasons why your price is a bargain! If your customer says, "This is too expensive," you may say, "That's the very reason you need to buy it! We've talked about your family's needs and how long you want it to last. This [product] is exactly what you need. Your budget is the very reason you need it." To state this confidently, recall the times you have considered two products, bought the cheaper one, and later regretted it. A bargain that doesn't deliver can become expensive. The bitterness of poor quality remains longer than the sweetness of low price.

- **Change the scale.** "Four dollars per square foot is a terrific value for carpet of this quality. You probably realize, from shopping around, that many other stores charge $6 a square foot, some even more, for carpet that doesn't have [insert a benefit to "brag" about the product]." Or say, "It is a lot of money, and it's worth every penny." Or use the surprise tactic when you believe the product costs less than comparable products. When she likes the product and expects you to name a price close to those higher-priced items, you can say, "This [product] is only $___, and it's worth every penny and then some!" Restate why the price is a bargain, using honesty and passion.

Or consider Joe McGuire's method. He sold Remington Rand® electric typewriters in a market dominated by IBM®. But he was convinced his typewriter was the best. He treated every comment by a customer as a compliment to his typewriter. When a prospect asked how much it cost, Joe would answer, "That's the best part about it—it's only $635." Some prospects were surprised, expecting a lower price. They would answer, "$635?" And confidently Joe would answer, "I knew you would be surprised. Most people would expect it to cost a great deal more than that." Joe believed it was a bargain, and that's why his customers began to see it as a bargain.

❤ **Use an affirmative defense.** Mention the price early in your presentation. At the close, restate all the benefits of the product and what it will do for the customer. Then move for the commitment, leaving out the price, and be silent. Wait for her to ask about price. When she asks, you could respond, "Yes, most people think it's a lot less than they imagined considering its benefits. [Specify them.]" If she sticks with the price issue, she's probably not emotionally committed to the product. Despite her protests, price may not be her real objection. Here's where you earn your paycheck by influencing her to want it at this price.

❤ **Never admit sameness.** Conceding sameness is giving away your competitive advantage. When you sell what customers consider a commodity, you must usually battle about price. The alternative is to not concede sameness. Sell the distinction of your products, services, company, and *you*. Even though the product is the same, your value package is not the same. "With this product, you get me and my store's reputation; it's not the same." Don't give away your competitive advantage.

In his book, *Purple Cow: Transform Your Business By Being Remarkable*, marketing guru Seth Godin talks about common cows. One looks pretty much like the others. But a purple cow would be remarkable! You would remark about it to your associates. You would go to see it again, take pictures, and maybe even bring your friends to see for themselves. To be "not the same," you need to find—you need to be—a purple cow.[65]

♥ **Build value.** When a customer says, "I can get it down the street cheaper," if you cave in and lower the price, you concede that the value of your offer didn't warrant your price. You also undermine your integrity. When you lower your price as a negotiating tactic, you lose your customer's trust. She thinks, "If you really cared so much about me, why didn't you offer me the best price at first?" To yourself, you must concede, "Okay, you caught me. Now I'll have to sell it to you for the real price!"

Don't lower the price, but rather stress the value: "We're worth more because of [state the benefits proudly and confidently]." Here's an example: "We're worth more because we use certified installers and give you a lifetime installation warranty. Does the other store offer that?" To do this well, of course, you must fully understand why your product is more valuable than your competitor's. If you don't, the customer certainly won't.

To feel the power of this value-adding method, imagine you are shopping in my store for a glass bowl. You see two identical-looking bowls, one priced at $5 and the other at $10. If you found no information about their quality, which one would you probably buy? You're about to pick up the cheaper one, but you see me and say, "These two glasses look identical. Are they?"

I respond, "No, this one is made of Austrian crystal and has a life-time guarantee. The other doesn't." Now how do you feel about their relative value and the price disparity? Does price fade as the decision-maker? Or are you weighing their relative quality?

Reader's Digest® once told a story about three pizza parlors situated on the same street in Brooklyn. In fact, they were next door to each other and competition was fierce. One store put up a sign: Best Pizza in all of New York! People flocked to it. Not to be out-done, a second store hung this sign: Best Pizza in all of America! People left the first store and came to the second in droves. Not to be outdone, the third pizza parlor came up with the definitive differentiation. Its sign read: Best Pizza on the Whole Block! He made the benefits up close and personal.

In another coup, two kids were selling lemonade in their neighborhood. One charged 50¢ and the other charged $1. The glasses looked as if they held the same amount, but one kid claimed his lemonade was worth twice as much. Why would he expect anyone to pay more? Because he promoted a benefit that might make his lemonade worth more. Beneath the $1 sign, he printed boldly: Ice cold! Thus, he could sell at a higher price, without stooping to discredit his competition.

Until you can show how your product or service will benefit your customer, any price will be too high. Customers buy at a price that reflects their perception of the product's value. It's your job to justify the price.

You can sell at prices higher than the competition when, in your heart, you believe your offer benefits customers as no other company's offer can. Most customers will believe your assessment, if you believe in the total value of your products and services, and if your integrity and that of your company exceed the price asked. If you don't believe that, you'll find yourself discussing price far too often. To minimize price-shopping, start believing in your value!

If you meet a true price-shopper, and you believe you must lower your price, do so only by subtracting something from your offer. "I could give you a lower price, but we will have to pull the CD player from the dash." Thus, you leave the customer empowered; she can choose whichever offer fulfills her current priority. And you defend the value of your original price. You lose neither credibility nor profit. Here are some other tactics to use with price-shoppers that will increase the likelihood of making the sale without hurting your credibility:

- ❤ I can lower the price, but I'll have to send Johnny. I couldn't do it myself.
- ❤ If you pay 100 percent cash up-front, I'll return the favor and give you a discount.
- ❤ Because you're buying this much product, we can get it cheaper from our supplier. We'll give you the savings.

But don't offer a volume discount if the store doesn't save money! Yes, I know you want this big order, and you hope this customer will tell other shoppers with potentially big orders. But if she tells them, she'll also tell them, "And they gave me a volume discount." So you've set the precedent and can't recover your loss. When you start negotiating price and word gets out, the game quickly changes. Customers wonder, "What tricks can I use to get the price down?"

In the end, it pays not to negotiate prices. The real question in most customers' minds is: "Am I getting my money's worth?"

Avoid the Product/Price Comparison Trap

Customers want to own superior products, especially large-ticket items. They want quality to avoid the hassle of inferior ones. As Lee Iacocca said, "People want economy and they will pay any price to get it."[66] Consequently, they will often ask you which of two similar products is good. They hope you will declare one as good and the other bad. Consumers like white/black differences. They want to feel smart buying the good one and outsmarting the lure of the bad one.

So beware of good versus bad comparisons. First, it's seldom true. Few products are "bad." Every product has limitations as well as advantages. Every product has a price for its benefits. Thus any "bad" evaluation would prove untrue. Think positively, as Napoleon Hill, author of *Think and Grow Rich*, recommended, "The super salesman does not permit his subconscious mind to 'broadcast' negative thoughts, nor does he express them through words…He understands that like attracts like, and negative suggestions attract negative action and decisions from prospective buyers."[67]

Second, if you're unsure about the function of a product, say so. To understand the effectiveness of this method, imagine going into a restaurant for the first time. As you're scanning the menu, you ask your server, "What's good?" If he says, "Everything's good," check to see if you're at the Marietta diner near my home north of Atlanta. If you are, relax! I testify it's all good. But if you're not, you might wonder if he's exaggerating. On the other hand, what if he says, "Well, I haven't tried everything on the menu, but I would recommend the lamb over the veal." How would your opinion of his credibility change?

Third, if you did declare a product "bad" or "inferior," you would risk belittling the alternative your customer favors.

And fourth, you never want to label a competitor's products as bad. Avoid black and white when the true relative merits are shades of gray.

Now, I'm not suggesting that you avoid comparison altogether. Just avoid "good and bad" comparisons. The comparisons of "good, better, and best" are usually closer to actuality. I'm also not saying that you must avoid mentioning the specific shortcomings of any product your customer considers.

Examples of positive comparisons:

- Well, some products work better in this application than others.
- I think this less expensive product is superior to the more expensive one when it is used for…
- One of the things you'll like more about this product is…

Being honest may increase your customer's trust, and she may accept your recommendations. Average salespeople promise anything to make a sale, but that doesn't increase trust.

As we've said, customers need to feel that you're willing to lose a sale rather than sell an ill-fitting product. The solution is to promote each product positively, for its intended uses, and on its own merits. Spend time reviewing the features and benefits of products with which you are unfamiliar, and the combination of features and benefits that differentiates each product. Learn to promote them positively. Then let the customer decide what she wants based on how she plans to use it and what's important to her.

In my experience, the vast majority of salespeople volunteered a price discount without being asked. That proves that the greatest obstacle to selling at the set price lies in the minds of salespeople, not buyers! It's salespeople who don't believe their products and services are worth the price. Their doubt usually stems from ignorance of their products' benefits, and the value that consumers place on those benefits.

Remember that price influences the purchase decision but rarely determines it.

There's No Such Thing as a Strike Out!

Let's take a moment to think about that great American pastime: No, not sales—baseball! Which statistics best represent a player's contribution? Total runs scored? Home runs? Batting average? As a retail storeowner, sales manager, or salesperson, which statistics do you think best measure the salesperson's contribution?

Sales revenue! Well, yes, that's important. But total sales don't tell you how efficiently your salespeople sell. They tell you the total, but not how often a salesperson sells per opportunity to sell. They are the equivalent of total hits, but not batting average. In sales, we call it "closing rate." As a sales manager, I learn more by knowing how efficiently each salesperson works. Here's why:

When a baseball player raises his batting average from .250 to .350, that's amazing—the stuff of sports-page headlines. Yet that achievement requires the player to hit only once more in 10 at-bats. One in 10 produces a 10-point improvement (from .250 to .350). If your company's salespeople raised their closing rate by one more in 10, how would such an improvement transform your store?

In retail, the average salesperson sells to one out of every four shoppers he or she talks to. That's an average closing rate of 25 percent. If the average salesperson could close one more out of 10 tries, the closing rate would rise by 10 percentage points (from 25 to 35 percent). If that happened in your store, would your sales rise by 10 percent? No. Much more!

Let's say your average closing rate is 25 percent and the average price of the products you sell is $1000; so, the average salesperson sells $2500 for every 10 shoppers. If your salespeople raised their average by 10 percentage points, to 35 percent, they would sell $3500. Climbing from 25 to 35 percent is not a 10 percent increase. It's a whopping 40 percent increase ($3500 divided by $2500)! This 10-point increase yields 40 percent more sales. That should increase the confidence and self-esteem of salespeople!

But unlike baseball that allows a batter three strikes, customers seldom offer salespeople a second or third chance. If you don't get a hit the first time, you're usually out. When your customer says, "I would like to think it over" or "This is the first place I've visited," do you consider yourself out? Don't. If you don't respond confidently at that point, it's like you didn't even take a swing! You just dropped the bat and walked back to the dugout.

The best "hitters"—master salespeople—figure out a way to get another swing at the customer, while average salespeople do nothing. If they miss on the first swing, they give up. I want you to think differently. In selling, it's not three strikes and you're out. You're out only when the customer tells you you're out. Until she does, I want you to keep on swinging. Try the following techniques used by big-league salespeople:

- ♥ They keep a running list of closed sales and potential sales. If, during a first visit, the customer doesn't buy (or commit to something), they figure a way to get her to return for a second "at-bat." They know closing rates skyrocket when customers return to the store. They give every potential customer second-, third-, and fourth-inning opportunities to buy from them.

- When a customer says, "I've got to shop around first," big-leaguers continue to sell. They offer something to convince her that she should stay in touch. They may say, "Mrs. Smith, if I think of something that might work for you, would it be okay if I called or emailed to tell you?" They get her name, address, telephone number, and email address.

- They create ways to constantly keep in touch—to get another swing at the customer. Meanwhile, average salespeople sit at their desks and wait—hoping a new customer will come in. Heart & Mind salespeople don't wait at their desks. They act.

- Most Heart & Mind salespeople send personal thank-you notes to the prior day's shoppers, both those who purchased and (especially) those who didn't. "Thanks for coming in. I enjoyed waiting on you. I wish you well as you search to find that perfect item. After you left, I thought of another product I should have showed you. If you haven't purchased yet, I would love to show it to you."

- Heart & Mind salespeople may even send prospects a gift—like a free video rental or tickets to a local baseball game, with a note that reads, "Thanks for coming by. I so enjoyed our visit. Please take your family out for some fun on me." Remember when we talked about gifts as a language of love? It couldn't hurt! And remember the power of the Law of Give and Take!

As the legendary Babe Ruth said, "Every strike brings me closer to the next home run."[68] You can't hit a home run unless you swing again. You can't close unless you ask. You can't reach your goals if you give up.

Signing the Loyalty Contract

Once the customer has consented to the agreement, you hope she'll relax. She'll feel relief and pleasure, even excitement. She'll be grateful and open to doing you a favor in return. At worst, she'll feel a tinge of worry: Did I do the right thing? Can we afford it? Will everyone like it?

As you write the order and discuss other terms, it's time to calm any fears and reassure her of the rightness of her choice. You may want to review the benefits, anticipate how much she will enjoy the product, and establish the delivery date.

Vow Your Loyalty to the Customer

You also want to assure the customer that your company stands behind her purchase. Restate all the product warranties and your company's policies on satisfaction. Add your personal pledge that you will assist with any questions or issues during ownership. Pledge to be her advocate. Let her see that you represent her interests (within the authority you have).

Thus, you want to vow your personal loyalty, your company's loyalty, and the manufacturer's loyalty to the customer. If the two of you feel a Heart & Mind connection, the customer will likely feel loyalty as well.

Invite the Customer to Vow Her Loyalty

You want to influence the customer to give voice to her feelings of loyalty to you and your company. You can describe how much you've enjoyed working with her, and that you would like to give the same loyal service to her friends: "To help me grow and progress, I would like to know your honest opinion. What do you think you'll tell your family and friends about how we worked together and found just what you wanted?"

Ask her for referrals—family or friends you might call. If your store offers a gift to customers who give referrals, offer her the prize. Your sales manager should have a full customer-referral program for you to follow.

If not, read books on selling and find a program you can recommend for your store.

A Final Word

If you follow my advice from the previous chapters, this step—signing the contract—will come naturally. When you have rightly built a Heart & Mind connection with the customer, and served her as a Heart & Mind salesperson should, you can expect her to vow her loyalty to you.

Voila! You have a new friend. And the puzzle is complete!

Chapter 21

Recap: How a Heart & Mind Sale Flows

"The secret of happiness is this: Let your interests be as whole as possible, and let your reactions to the things and persons that interest you be as far as possible friendly rather than hostile."

—Bertrand Russell,
British author, mathematician, and philospoher

You lead, but you don't dominate. You and the customer co-lead: You guide the *process*; the customer guides the *content*.

You gain power to lead the customer by virtue of who you are and how you *act*.

You take the customer as she is. If she's not like you, you can't mold her into your ideal. You can, however, influence how the customer responds to you. You can affect what she feels and thinks. Then the customer's feelings and thoughts will determine how she acts.

Thus, by applying Heart & Mind Selling, you induce the customer to correspond. Here's the process:

1. As the customer enters store, you are her *adversary*.
2. As she warms to you, she adopts you as her *advisor*.
3. When she buys, she considers you her *advocate*.

Now let's summarize your actions and the customer's responding feelings, thoughts, and actions. I hope it helps you see how you might structure your ideal sales conversation.

You Lead		Customer Responds	
You are...	**Therefore, you...**	**Customer feels and thinks...**	**Therefore, customer...**
Amiable	Are warm and hospitable. Have a *familiar* sociability. Seek commonalities.	*This salesperson is easy to talk with. I think we're going to be compatible.*	Drops some of her social defenses.
Good-willed	Show a kindly interest in your customer's physical and emotional comfort. Offer the customer the full resources of the company and its showroom of products. Propose to guide the customer to find what she wants.	*This is so different from the last store I shopped! The salesperson wants to help me get what I want. Buying is hard enough without fighting a pushy salesperson.*	Listens to you. Is kindly disposed toward you.

You Lead		Customer Responds	
You are...	**Therefore, you...**	**Customer feels and thinks...**	**Therefore, customer...**
Respectful	Respect the customer. Ask permission before you do anything. Invite the customer to be open and candid with you. Invite *two*-way openness and influence. Ask questions instead of telling.	*The salesperson must realize who I am. The salesperson believes I'm important. The salesperson values my opinions and believes that I can select the best product, with his/her help. The salesperson will listen to me, so I can influence him/her. The salesperson won't run over me.*	Respects you. Reveals her desires and needs. Has empathy for you.
Harmonic	Avoid sense of opposition and argument. Match her manner, words, pace, style. Use humor. Touch her appropriately. Cheer her up.	*The salesperson likes me just as I am. I can be myself with him/her. The salesperson is relaxed, the kind of person I like to work with.*	Opens her natural self.

You Lead		Customer Responds	
You are…	**Therefore, you…**	**Customer feels and thinks…**	**Therefore, customer…**
Goal-Directed and Ego-Driven	Take initiative to search for products and services that fully suit her desires.	*We're going to get this done today! Hurray! I think I'll get a product that I'll like for years.*	Engages herself in the search because you have captured her imagination.
Caring	Strive to build rapport. Ask questions to draw out her *real* desires.	*The salesperson wants me to buy what I want! The salesperson likes my tastes. I can tell him/her my dreams for this room.*	Responds fully to questions. Jointly leads the product hunt.
Competent	Know products, procedures, competition, etc.	*The salesperson knows what he/she is talking about! I didn't realize all the factors I need to consider when buying this. I'm so lucky to have found this salesperson.*	Gains confidence in sales credibility.
Articulate	Explain everything with clarity, relevance, simplicity, and efficiency.	*I think I understand this stuff. I never thought I would.*	Listens more carefully. Does not misinterpret your statements.

You Lead		Customer Responds	
You are...	Therefore, you...	Customer feels and thinks...	Therefore, customer...
Empathetic	Show you understand the customer's desires by presenting only products that tie to her specific situation.	*It's amazing! The salesperson actually understands what I want. I think I'll like what I buy, because it'll reflect me—the best of me.*	Has confidence in your value judgments and heeds them. Gains confidence in her own growing expertise.
Biased toward the best outcome for the customer and company	Show no bias *against* the customer's interests, such as seeking a commission or pushing a particular product. Seek an agreement that pleases both the customer and your company.	*Looks like the salesperson won't be pushing any products on me today. The salesperson is supporting me in this search. Thank goodness!*	Forgets wariness. Warms to you and your company.
Honest	Tell facts accurately. Use only true statements.	*The salesperson's telling me the truth, and the whole truth. It's incredible, the salesperson's so credible!*	Believes your facts.

You Lead		Customer Responds	
You are…	**Therefore, you…**	**Customer feels and thinks…**	**Therefore, customer…**
Trustworthy	Keep promises. Align your principles and actions with the customer's. Don't exaggerate judgments.	*The salesperson is not the "usual" salesperson. The salesperson can see both sides. The salesperson will back up what he/she says.*	Trusts you. Relies on your promises.
Trusting of the customer	Trust the customer's statements and value her judgments.	*The salesperson thinks I have good judgment. I like that.*	Acts openly and confidently.
Open	Give opinions candidly and tactfully. Recognize the pros and cons of *all* products.	*You know, I think the salesperson is right. The salesperson makes a lot of sense. There are a lot more good choices than I would have thought. I'm glad I have this salesperson.*	Tells you her real reactions and objections. Trusts you more.

You Lead		Customer Responds	
You are...	**Therefore, you...**	**Customer feels and thinks...**	**Therefore, customer...**
Enthusiastic	Propose a purchase.	*Yes, that product is best for me. I know it costs a bit more, and it doesn't have this or that, but it's the best one, and I'll be happy with it. I agree with the salesperson. Oh, yes! I'm so pleased.*	Has confidence in your judgment and accepts your proposal. Has the Enthusiasm and Ego-Drive to sign the contract. Anticipates enjoying the product.
In affinity with customer	Sign the contract on behalf of the company and yourself. Vow resources and loyalty to the customer.	*This has been a great experience— much easier than I was expecting. I'm going to enjoy our relationship in the future. I've got to tell my family and friends about this place...and this salesperson!*	Vows mutual loyalty to you and the store because of her experience. Becomes a cheerleader for you and your company. Refers friends and family. Returns to buy again and again.

At the End, Heart & Mind Salespeople Don't *Close*, They *Open*

When the customer says yes, it's not the close—it's the opening of a relationship for life. Heart & Mind Selling looks like this:

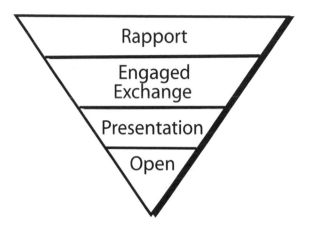

The "open" is the culmination of all the other steps put together. You built rapport with the customer, you spent time in an engaged exchange that allowed you to care about and trust each other, you focused on benefits important to the customer, and you demonstrated your product the way the customer wanted and needed it demonstrated.

But remember, you didn't just make a Heart & Mind *transaction*—you made a Heart & Mind *connection*, a connection built on mutual trust, affinity, rapport, and loyalty that will lead to a personally (and financially!) fulfilling relationship between you and your customer.

Good luck, and happy selling!

About the Author

Sam Allman's reputation as a compelling speaker and results-oriented consultant was earned through more than 50 years of retail sales experience. Using his expertise, and working with companies like The Home Depot® and SEARS®, Allman has created the system he describes in this book: **Heart & Mind Selling**. This innovative approach has created considerable buzz in the sales world and has proven to boost sales and retain customers.

Allman began his career in sales on the ground floor—literally—as a 9-year-old helping his father install carpeting for the family business. Since then, he has owned his own flooring company, been a top-producing salesman at two prominent retail distributors, and was recruited to become Vice President of Total Quality Training and Development for Mohawk Industries in Atlanta. In 1995, he became the Dean of Mohawk University, a corporate training institution, and was responsible for creating the entire sales training curriculum for the university.

For the last two decades, Allman has delivered customized, high-quality content, inspiring programs in areas such as leadership, customer service, management development, team building, retail sales, and personal quality management. Allman has made presentations to The Home Depot®, SEARS®, Novell® and the Health Trust Corporation®, among others, and appeared in *The Wall Street Journal* and *Selling Power*. He frequently contributes to *National Floor Trends*, *Mohawk Kaleidoscope*, *Western Reporter*, and the publications of the National Home Furnishing Association and the National Association of Floor Covering Distributors. He is also the author of several books, and *The Art of Retail Management*, an essay widely read in the retail industry.

Today, Allman serves as President of **Allman Consulting and Training**, a firm providing sales training and consulting to Fortune 500 companies and continues to apply the Heart & Mind Approach in his own life. He and his wife, Jessie, have 10 children and 15 grandchildren.

For more on Allman's services, please visit *www.SamAllmanSpeaks.com.*

End Notes

1. Stark, Peter B. *The Only Negotiating Guide You'll Ever Need: 101 Ways to Win Every Time in Any Situation* (New York, NY: Broadway Books, 2003).
2. Tracy, Brian. *Advanced Selling Strategies: The Proven System of Sales Ideas, Methods, and Techniques Used by Top Salespeople Everywhere* (New York, NY: Simon & Schuster Inc., 1996).
3. Greenberg, Herbert M. and David Mayer. "What Makes a Good Salesman?" *Harvard Business Review*, (2006).
4. Fleming, John H. "Why Consistency is the Key to Profitable Customer Service," (August 10th, 2006), http://gmj.gallup.com/content/default.aspx?ci=23953&pg=2 (accessed October 2006).
5. CyberNation, "Niels Bohr," http://www.cybernation.com/quotationcenter/quoteshow.php?id=40192 (accessed October 2006).
6. *Glengarry Glen Ross*, DVD. Directed by James Foley. 1993, Los Angeles, CA: Lion's Gate, 2002.
7. Coffman, Curt, Fleming, John, and James K. Harter, "Manage Your Human Stigma." *Harvard Business Review*, (July-August, 2005).
8. Fresh Thinking Business, "Sam Walton Biography," http://freshthinkingbusiness.com/sam-walton.html (accessed October 2006).
9. Disend, Jeffrey. *How to Provide Excellent Service in Any Organization.* (West Chester, PA: Chilton Book Company, 1991).
10. Mayeroff, Milton. *On Caring.* (New York, NY: Harper & Row Publishers, 1971).
11. Mayeroff, Milton. "Earn Customer Loyalty the Hard Way." *Selling Power*, (April 2006).

12. Carbone, Lewis. *Clued In: How to Keep Customers Coming Back Again and Again.* (Upper Saddle River, NJ: Financial Times Prentice Hall, 2004).

13. Chapman, Gary D. *The Five Languages of Love: How to Express Heartfelt Commitment to Your Mate.* (Chicago: Northfield Publishing, 1995).

14. Crusco, April H. and Christopher G. Wetzel, "The Midas Touch: The Effects of Interpersonal Touch on Restaurant Tipping" *Personality and Social Psychology Bulletin, Vol. 10, No. 4,* (1984): 512-517.

15. Tolnspire Quotes, "Harry Emerson Fosdick," http://www.atozquotes.com/author.asp?author=Harry+Emerson+Fosdick (accessed October 2006).

16. Lewis, Jordan D. *The Connected Corporation.* (New York: Free Press, 1996).

17. Mooney, Kelly. *"The Ten Demandments: Rules to Live By in The Age of the Demanding Customer"* (New York, NY: McGraw-Hill Companies, July 2002.)

18. Answers.com, "Bear Bryant: Information from Answers.com," http://www.answers.com/topic/paul-bryant (accessed October 2006).

19. Reh, John F. "Pareto's Principle The 80-20 Rule," http://management.about.com/cs/generalmanagement/a/Pareto081202.htm (accessed October 2006).

20. Zaada Beta, "R.H. Grant Quotes," http://quotes.zaadz.com/R_H_Grant (accessed October 2006).

21. Senge, Peter M. *The Fifth Discipline.* (New York, NY: Doubleday, 1990).

22. Jones, H. "Valuable Insights from the Original Management Guru, the Late Peter Drucker" (25/10/2005). http://www.secondpost.com/Main/news/newsPopup.aspx?newsid=6609 (accessed October 2006).

23. "Quotations by Eleanor Roosevelt." Eleanor Roosevelt National Historical Site http://www.nps.gov/archive/elro/who-is-er/er-quotes/ (accessed October 2006).

24. Monson, Thomas S. *Favorite Quotations from the Collection of Thomas S. Monson.* (Salt Lake City, UT: Deseret Book Company, 1985).

25. Deming, Edwards W. *Out of the Crisis.* (Cambridge, MA: MIT Press, 1982).

26. Reh, John F. "Pareto's Principle: The 80-20 Rule," http://management.about.com/cs/generalmanagement/a/Pareto081202.htm (accessed October 2006).

27. Zaada Beta, "Quotes about Sales," http://quotes.zaadz.com/topics/sales (accessed October 2006).

28. Rogers, Carl R. and Kramer, Peter D. *On Becoming a Person: A Therapist's View of Psychotherapy.* (Boston, MA: Mariner Books, 1995).

29. Covey, Stephen R. *The 7 Habits of Highly Effective People.* (New York, NY: Free Press, 1990).

30. Tournier, Paul. *To Understand Each Other.* (Louisville, KY: Westminster John Knox Press, 2000).

31. "StarChild: Meteoroids," NASA http:starchild.gsfc.nasa.gov/docs/StarChild/solar_system_level2/meteoroids.html (accessed October 2006).

32. "Orison Swett Marden Quotes," ThinkExist.com, http://en.thinkexist.com/quotes/orison_swett_marden/ (accessed October 2006).

33. James, William. *William James: Writings 1878-1899: Psychology, Briefer Course / The Will to Believe / Talks to Teachers and Students / Essays* (New York, NY: Library of America, 1992).

34. Rosener, Judy. *America's Competitive Secret: Women Managers.* New York, NY: Oxford University Press, 1995).

35. Interep. 2003. *"All about Women: Demographic, Spending,*

and Media Profiles: Marketing Strategies to Target Female Consumers" New York, NY: Interep. (Based on Fall 2002 findings by MediaMark Research Inc.)

36.   "It's Time to Cut to the Chase, Men: Wives Are the Key to What We Buy" *Atlanta Journal-Constitution*, (October 23, 2005). www. newslibrary.com/sites/ajc (accessed October 2006).

37.   Fun Loving Time, "Delinquent Taxes 2005 View this year's local delinquent tax sale report. No matter how you… The Wife Factor…" (October 10, 2005) http://www.funlovetime.com/ node/147 (accessed October 2006).

38.   Barletta, Martha. *Marketing to Women: How to Understand, Reach, and Increase Your Share of the World's Largest Market Segment.* (New York, NY: Kaplan Business, 2005).

39.   Peters, Tom. "Everything You Need to Know About Strategy: A Baker's Dozen Eternal Verities," (October 18th, 2004) http://www. tompeters.com/blogs/freestuff/uploads/StrategyBakersDozen10180 4.pdf (accessed October 2006).

40.   Peters, Tom. "Everything You Need to Know About Strategy: A Baker's Dozen Eternal Verities," (October 18th, 2004) http://www. tompeters.com/blogs/freestuff/uploads/StrategyBakersDozen10180 4.pdf (accessed October 2006).

41.   Silverstein, Michael. And Neil Fiske, *Trading Up: The New American Luxury* (New York, NY: The Penguin Group, 2003).

42.   "Facts about Working Women", Indiana University. http://www. homepages.indiana.edu/031204/text/women2.html (accessed October 2006).

43.   Silverstein, Michael. And Neil Fiske, *Trading Up: The New American Luxury* (New York, NY: The Penguin Group, 2003).

44.   Colin Carmen V., Simons, George F. and Vasquez, Carmen. *Transcultural Leadership: Empowering the Diverse Workforce.* (Atlanta, GA: Gulf Professional Publishing, 2006).

45.   Popcorn, Faith, and Lys Marigold. *Clicking: 17 Trends that Drive*

Your Business and Your Life, (New York, NY: HarperCollins Publishers, 1997).

46. Quinlan, Mary Lou. *Just Ask a Woman: Cracking the Code of What Women Want and How They Buy.* (Hoboken, NJ: Wiley, 2003).

47. "What is NLP," Neuro-linguistic Programming, http://www.nlp.com/whatisnlp.aspx (accessed October 2006).

48. *Star Wars*, Directed by George Lucas. 1977, Las Angeles, CA: 20th Century Fox, 1997.

49. Cialdini, Robert. *Influence: The Psychology of Persuasion.* (New York, NY: Collins, 1998).

50. Cialdini, Robert. *Influence: The Psychology of Persuasion.* (New York, NY: Collins, 1998).

51. Lincoln, Abraham & Don E. Fehrenbacher. *Abraham Lincoln: A Documentary Portrait Through His Speeches and Writings.* (Stanford, CA: Stanford University Press, 1964).

52. *Sideways*, DVD. Directed by Alexander Payne. 2004, Los Angeles, CA: 20th Century Fox, 2004.

53. Carnegie, Dale. *How to Win Friends & Influence People.* (New York, NY: Pocket, 1990).

54. Brooks, Bill, and Tom Travisano, *You're Working Too Hard to Make the Sale!* (Columbus, OH: McGraw-Hill Companies, 1995).

55. Epictetus. *The Art of Living: The Classic Manuel on Virtue, Happiness and Effectiveness.* (San Francisco, CA: Harper San Francisco, 2004).

56. "Creative Quotations from Dean Rusk(1909-1994)," Creative Quotations, http://creativequotations.com/one/742.htm (accessed October 2006).

57. Fisher, Annie. "Willy Loman Couldn't Cut It," *Fortune*, no. 22 (November 11, 1996).

58. Nichols, Ralph G. *Listening and Speaking: A Guide to Effective Oral Communication.* (Dubuque, IA: WC Brown, 1954).

59. Fries, Charles C. "Implications of Modern Linguistic Science".

College English, Volume 8 Number 6, (March, 1947).

60. Fripp, Patricia. "Patricia Fripp's Frippicisms," www.fripp.com/frippicismbest.html (accessed October 2006).

61. Brooks, Bill, and Tom Travisano, *You're Working Too Hard to Make the Sale!* (Columbus, OH: McGraw-Hill Companies, 1995).

62. Carnegie, Dale. *How to Win Friends & Influence People.* (New York, NY: Pocket, 1990).

63. "Right Brain vs. Left Brain," Funderstanding. http://www.funderstanding.com/right_left_brain.cfm (accessed October 2006).

64. ThinkExist.com, "Wayne Gretzky Quotes,"http://en.thinkexist.com/quotation/you_miss-of_the_shots_you_don-t_take/15171.html (accessed October 2006).

65. Godin, Seth. *Purple Cow: Transform Your Business By Being Remarkable.* (New York, NY: Penguin Group, 2003).

66. Salpukas, Agis. "Detroit Faces '75 Fit for Any Shift; Detroit Faces '75 Fit for Shift," *New York Times.* (October 13, 1974) Section: SA, Page 1.

67. Hill, Napoleon. *Think and Grow Rich: The Andrew Carnegie Formula for Money Making.* (New York, NY: Random House, 1996).

68. "Quotes by Babe Ruth," The Official Babe Ruth Website, http://www.baberuth.com/flash/about/quotes.html (accessed October 2006).

69. "B.C. Forbes," Cybernation.com, http://www.cybernation.com/quotationcenter/quoteshow.php?type=author&id=3108 (accessed October 2006).